50 Italian Dessert Recipes for Home

By: Kelly Johnson

Table of Contents

- Tiramisu
- Cannoli
- Panna Cotta
- Gelato
- Biscotti
- Sfogliatella
- Zabaglione
- Cassata
- Zeppole
- Amaretti
- Semifreddo
- Budino
- Crostata
- Ricotta Cheesecake
- Panettone
- Pandoro
- Struffoli
- Zuppa Inglese
- Bomboloni
- Torta Caprese
- Pizzelle
- Torta della Nonna
- Maritozzi
- Torrone
- Granita
- Frittelle di Carnevale
- Biscotti Regina
- Torta Mimosa
- Croccante
- Mostaccioli
- Fiadone
- Pinolata
- Panforte
- Tartufo
- Sbrisolona

- Castagnaccio
- Baci di Dama
- Brutti ma Buoni
- Ciambellone
- Cantucci
- Torta di Mele
- Torta Paradiso
- Baba al Limoncello
- Ricciarelli
- Biancomangiare
- Gubana
- Bustrengo
- Migliaccio
- Pignolata
- Sanguinaccio Dolce

Tiramisu

Ingredients:

- 6 large egg yolks
- 3/4 cup granulated sugar
- 1 cup mascarpone cheese, softened
- 1 1/2 cups heavy cream
- 1 teaspoon vanilla extract
- 2 cups strong brewed coffee, cooled
- 1/4 cup coffee liqueur (optional)
- 1 package (about 7 ounces) ladyfingers (savoiardi)
- Cocoa powder, for dusting

Instructions:

1. Prepare the Coffee Mixture:
    - Brew strong coffee and let it cool to room temperature. Stir in the coffee liqueur, if using.
2. Make the Mascarpone Mixture:
    - In a large mixing bowl, whisk together the egg yolks and sugar until pale and creamy.
    - Add the softened mascarpone cheese and vanilla extract to the egg mixture, and whisk until smooth and well combined.
    - In a separate bowl, whip the heavy cream until stiff peaks form. Gently fold the whipped cream into the mascarpone mixture until smooth and creamy.
3. Assemble the Tiramisu:
    - Quickly dip each ladyfinger into the coffee mixture, ensuring they are well soaked but not soggy.
    - Arrange a layer of soaked ladyfingers in the bottom of a 9x13-inch baking dish or a trifle dish.
    - Spread half of the mascarpone mixture over the soaked ladyfingers, smoothing it out with a spatula.
    - Repeat with another layer of soaked ladyfingers and the remaining mascarpone mixture.
4. Chill the Tiramisu:
    - Cover the tiramisu with plastic wrap and refrigerate for at least 4 hours, or preferably overnight, to allow the flavors to meld and the dessert to set.
5. Serve:

- Before serving, dust the top of the tiramisu with cocoa powder using a fine-mesh sieve.
- Slice and serve the chilled tiramisu with a cup of espresso or coffee.

Tips:

- For a non-alcoholic version, you can omit the coffee liqueur or replace it with additional coffee.
- Make sure to use room temperature mascarpone cheese for easier blending.
- Allow the tiramisu to chill in the refrigerator for at least 4 hours, but overnight is best, as it allows the flavors to develop and the dessert to set properly.
- Tiramisu is best served cold straight from the refrigerator.

Enjoy this classic Italian dessert with its rich coffee flavor and creamy texture. It's perfect for special occasions or anytime you crave a decadent treat!

Cannoli

Ingredients:

For the Cannoli Shells:

- 2 cups all-purpose flour, plus extra for dusting
- 2 tablespoons granulated sugar
- 1/4 teaspoon salt
- 2 tablespoons unsalted butter, softened
- 1/2 cup white wine or Marsala wine
- 1 large egg, beaten (for egg wash)
- Vegetable oil, for frying

For the Ricotta Filling:

- 2 cups whole milk ricotta cheese, drained if necessary
- 1/2 cup powdered sugar, sifted
- 1 teaspoon vanilla extract
- 1/4 cup chopped pistachios or mini chocolate chips (optional, for garnish)
- Powdered sugar, for dusting

Instructions:

1. Make the Cannoli Dough:
    - In a large mixing bowl, combine the flour, granulated sugar, and salt. Add the softened butter and mix until the mixture resembles coarse crumbs.
    - Gradually add the white wine or Marsala wine, mixing until a dough forms. Knead the dough on a lightly floured surface until smooth and elastic.
    - Wrap the dough in plastic wrap and let it rest at room temperature for about 30 minutes.
2. Roll out and Cut the Dough:
    - Divide the rested dough into two portions. Roll out each portion of dough on a lightly floured surface until very thin, about 1/8 inch thick.
    - Using a round cutter or a glass, cut out circles of dough. The size of the circles will depend on the size of your cannoli molds. Wrap each circle of dough around a metal cannoli tube, overlapping the edges slightly, and press to seal.
3. Fry the Cannoli Shells:

- In a large, deep pot, heat vegetable oil to 350°F (175°C). Carefully fry the cannoli shells in batches until golden brown and crisp, about 3-4 minutes.
- Use tongs to remove the fried shells from the oil and place them on paper towels to drain and cool. Once cooled, carefully slide the shells off the metal tubes and set them aside to cool completely.

4. Make the Ricotta Filling:
   - In a mixing bowl, combine the ricotta cheese, powdered sugar, and vanilla extract. Mix until smooth and creamy. Stir in chopped pistachios or mini chocolate chips, if using.
5. Fill the Cannoli Shells:
   - Just before serving, use a piping bag or spoon to fill the cooled cannoli shells with the ricotta filling. Fill each shell from both ends to ensure even distribution of the filling.
6. Serve:
   - Dust the filled cannoli with powdered sugar and garnish with additional chopped pistachios or mini chocolate chips, if desired.
   - Serve the cannoli immediately to enjoy them at their best.

Tips:

- It's best to fill the cannoli shells just before serving to prevent them from becoming soggy.
- If you don't have cannoli tubes, you can use metal or wooden dowels wrapped in aluminum foil as makeshift molds.
- Store any leftover filled cannoli shells in the refrigerator, but be aware that the shells may soften over time due to the moisture from the filling.

Enjoy these homemade cannoli with their crispy shells and creamy ricotta filling for a delightful taste of Italy!

Panna Cotta

Ingredients:

- 2 cups heavy cream
- 1/2 cup whole milk
- 1/2 cup granulated sugar
- 2 teaspoons vanilla extract
- 2 packets (14 grams) powdered gelatin
- 1/4 cup cold water

Instructions:

1. Prepare the Gelatin:
    - In a small bowl, sprinkle the powdered gelatin over the cold water. Let it sit for about 5-10 minutes to bloom and soften.
2. Heat the Cream Mixture:
    - In a saucepan, combine the heavy cream, whole milk, and granulated sugar. Heat the mixture over medium heat, stirring occasionally, until it just begins to simmer. Do not let it boil.
3. Dissolve the Gelatin:
    - Once the cream mixture is hot, remove it from the heat. Add the bloomed gelatin to the hot cream mixture and stir until the gelatin is completely dissolved.
4. Add Vanilla:
    - Stir in the vanilla extract until well combined.
5. Pour into Molds:
    - Lightly grease six ramekins or dessert cups with non-stick cooking spray. Pour the panna cotta mixture evenly into the prepared molds.
6. Chill and Set:
    - Place the filled molds in the refrigerator to chill for at least 4 hours, or until completely set. For best results, chill overnight.
7. Unmold and Serve:
    - Once the panna cotta is set, run a knife around the edges of each mold to loosen the dessert. Place a serving plate on top of each mold and quickly invert it to release the panna cotta onto the plate.
8. Serve:
    - Serve the panna cotta chilled, either on its own or with fresh berries, fruit compote, or a drizzle of caramel sauce.

Tips:

- For a richer flavor, you can infuse the cream mixture with other flavorings such as citrus zest, cinnamon, or coffee beans.
- Make sure to bloom the gelatin properly to ensure it dissolves completely and sets the panna cotta properly.
- You can adjust the sweetness of the panna cotta by varying the amount of sugar according to your taste preferences.
- If you prefer a lighter version, you can substitute part of the heavy cream with milk or even use coconut milk for a dairy-free option.

Enjoy this creamy and luxurious Italian dessert that's sure to impress your guests with its simplicity and elegance!

Gelato

Ingredients:

- 2 cups whole milk
- 1 cup heavy cream
- 3/4 cup granulated sugar
- 4 large egg yolks
- Flavorings of your choice (e.g., vanilla extract, cocoa powder, fruit puree, chopped nuts, espresso, etc.)

Instructions:

1. Prepare the Base:
    - In a saucepan, combine the whole milk, heavy cream, and granulated sugar. Heat the mixture over medium heat, stirring occasionally, until it just begins to simmer. Do not let it boil.
2. Temper the Egg Yolks:
    - While the milk mixture is heating, whisk the egg yolks in a separate bowl until smooth. Once the milk mixture is hot, gradually pour a small amount of it into the egg yolks while whisking constantly. This tempers the egg yolks and prevents them from curdling when added to the hot liquid.
3. Combine and Cook:
    - Pour the tempered egg yolk mixture back into the saucepan with the remaining hot milk mixture. Cook the mixture over medium-low heat, stirring constantly with a wooden spoon or silicone spatula, until it thickens slightly and coats the back of the spoon. This will take about 5-7 minutes. Do not let it boil.
4. Flavor the Base:
    - Once the mixture has thickened, remove it from the heat and stir in your desired flavorings. For example, add vanilla extract for vanilla gelato, cocoa powder for chocolate gelato, fruit puree for fruit-flavored gelato, etc. Stir until the flavorings are fully incorporated into the base.
5. Chill the Base:
    - Pour the gelato base through a fine-mesh sieve into a clean bowl to remove any lumps or bits of egg that may have formed. Cover the bowl with plastic wrap, pressing it directly onto the surface of the base to prevent a skin from forming. Chill the base in the refrigerator for at least 4 hours, or preferably overnight, until completely cold.

6. Churn the Gelato:
   - Once the gelato base is thoroughly chilled, pour it into an ice cream maker and churn according to the manufacturer's instructions until it reaches a soft, creamy consistency. This typically takes about 20-30 minutes.
7. Freeze:
   - Transfer the churned gelato to a freezer-safe container and freeze for an additional 2-4 hours, or until it firms up to your desired consistency.
8. Serve:
   - Scoop the gelato into bowls or cones and serve immediately. Enjoy your homemade gelato!

Tips:

- Experiment with different flavor combinations to create your own unique gelato recipes.
- For an extra smooth texture, strain the gelato base through a fine-mesh sieve before chilling.
- Store any leftover gelato in an airtight container in the freezer for up to two weeks. Allow it to soften slightly at room temperature for a few minutes before scooping and serving.

Making gelato at home allows you to customize the flavor and texture to your liking, resulting in a delicious frozen treat that's perfect for any occasion!

Biscotti

Ingredients:

- 2 cups all-purpose flour
- 1 cup granulated sugar
- 1 teaspoon baking powder
- 1/4 teaspoon salt
- 3 large eggs
- 1 teaspoon vanilla extract
- 1 teaspoon almond extract
- 1 cup whole almonds, toasted and roughly chopped

Instructions:

1. Preheat the Oven:
    - Preheat your oven to 350°F (175°C). Line a baking sheet with parchment paper or a silicone baking mat.
2. Mix Dry Ingredients:
    - In a large mixing bowl, whisk together the all-purpose flour, granulated sugar, baking powder, and salt until well combined.
3. Combine Wet Ingredients:
    - In a separate bowl, beat the eggs with the vanilla extract and almond extract until smooth.
4. Form Dough:
    - Gradually add the wet ingredients to the dry ingredients, mixing until a dough forms. Fold in the toasted and chopped almonds until evenly distributed.
5. Shape the Dough:
    - Divide the dough in half. On a lightly floured surface, shape each portion of dough into a log about 12 inches long and 2 inches wide. Place the logs on the prepared baking sheet, leaving space between them.
6. Bake First Time:
    - Bake the logs in the preheated oven for 25-30 minutes, or until lightly golden brown and firm to the touch. Remove from the oven and let cool on the baking sheet for 10 minutes.
7. Slice the Biscotti:
    - Using a serrated knife, slice the baked logs diagonally into 1/2-inch thick slices. Arrange the slices cut-side down on the baking sheet.

8. Bake Second Time:
    - Return the sliced biscotti to the oven and bake for an additional 10-15 minutes, or until golden brown and crispy. Remove from the oven and let cool completely on a wire rack.
9. Serve or Store:
    - Once cooled, the biscotti are ready to enjoy. Serve them as is or dip them in coffee, tea, or dessert wine. Store any leftover biscotti in an airtight container at room temperature for up to two weeks.

Tips:

- You can customize the flavor of your biscotti by adding other mix-ins such as chocolate chips, dried fruit, or citrus zest.
- For extra flavor, you can toast the almonds before adding them to the dough. Simply spread the almonds on a baking sheet and toast in the preheated oven for 8-10 minutes, or until fragrant and lightly golden brown.
- Biscotti can be made ahead of time and stored in an airtight container until ready to serve. They also make great homemade gifts during the holidays or for special occasions.

Sfogliatella

Ingredients:

For the Dough:

- 2 cups all-purpose flour
- 1/4 teaspoon salt
- 1/2 cup unsalted butter, cold and cubed
- 1/2 cup cold water

For the Filling:

- 1 cup whole milk ricotta cheese, drained if necessary
- 1/4 cup granulated sugar
- Zest of 1 lemon or orange
- 1/4 teaspoon ground cinnamon (optional)
- 1 large egg, beaten (for egg wash)
- Powdered sugar, for dusting

Instructions:

1. Make the Dough:
    - In a large mixing bowl, combine the all-purpose flour and salt. Add the cold, cubed butter and use a pastry cutter or your fingers to cut the butter into the flour until the mixture resembles coarse crumbs.
    - Gradually add the cold water, mixing until a rough dough forms. Turn the dough out onto a lightly floured surface and knead it gently until smooth. Wrap the dough in plastic wrap and refrigerate for at least 30 minutes.
2. Prepare the Filling:
    - In a separate bowl, mix together the ricotta cheese, granulated sugar, citrus zest, and ground cinnamon (if using) until well combined. Set aside.
3. Roll Out the Dough:
    - Preheat your oven to 375°F (190°C). On a lightly floured surface, roll out the chilled dough into a thin rectangle, about 1/8 inch thick.
4. Shape the Sfogliatella:
    - Spread a thin layer of the ricotta filling evenly over the rolled-out dough. Starting from one long edge, carefully roll the dough into a tight log. Use a sharp knife to cut the log into slices about 1 inch thick.
5. Form the Sfogliatella:

- Take each slice and gently press down on it with your palm to flatten it slightly. Then, using your fingers, gently stretch and pull the dough outward to form a thin oval shape with a raised edge in the center.

6. Bake:
    - Place the shaped sfogliatelle on a parchment-lined baking sheet. Brush the tops with beaten egg wash.
    - Bake in the preheated oven for 25-30 minutes, or until the sfogliatelle are golden brown and crispy.
7. Serve:
    - Remove the baked sfogliatelle from the oven and let them cool slightly on the baking sheet. Dust with powdered sugar before serving.

Tips:

- The dough for sfogliatelle can be quite delicate, so handle it gently to avoid tearing.
- If desired, you can add chopped candied citrus peel or chocolate chips to the ricotta filling for extra flavor and texture.
- Sfogliatelle are best enjoyed fresh on the day they are made, but they can be stored in an airtight container at room temperature for up to 2 days. Reheat them in the oven briefly before serving if desired.

Zabaglione

Ingredients:

- 4 large egg yolks
- 1/4 cup granulated sugar
- 1/2 cup Marsala wine (or another sweet wine such as Vin Santo or Moscato)
- Fresh fruit, cake, or biscuits for serving (optional)

Instructions:

1. Prepare a Double Boiler:
    - Fill a saucepan with a few inches of water and bring it to a simmer over medium heat. Place a heatproof bowl on top of the saucepan, ensuring that the bottom of the bowl does not touch the water. This setup creates a double boiler.
2. Whisk Egg Yolks and Sugar:
    - In the heatproof bowl, whisk together the egg yolks and granulated sugar until well combined and slightly pale in color.
3. Add Wine:
    - Gradually pour the Marsala wine into the egg yolk mixture while whisking constantly to combine.
4. Heat and Whisk:
    - Place the bowl over the simmering water in the saucepan, making sure the water does not touch the bottom of the bowl. Cook the zabaglione mixture, whisking constantly, until it thickens and becomes frothy. This will take about 8-10 minutes. The zabaglione should coat the back of a spoon and have a silky texture.
5. Serve Warm or Chilled:
    - Once the zabaglione is cooked to the desired consistency, remove it from the heat. Serve it warm immediately, or transfer it to a bowl and let it cool slightly before serving chilled.
6. Serve with Accompaniments:
    - Serve the zabaglione on its own in small bowls or glasses, or use it as a topping for fresh fruit, cake, or biscuits. You can also dust the top with cocoa powder or grated chocolate for extra flavor.

Tips:

- Be careful not to overcook the zabaglione, as it can curdle or become too thick. Remove it from the heat as soon as it reaches the desired consistency.
- If you prefer a lighter zabaglione, you can substitute part of the Marsala wine with another liquid such as fruit juice or coffee.
- Zabaglione is best enjoyed immediately after cooking, but it can be stored in the refrigerator for up to 24 hours. If chilled, let it come to room temperature before serving for the best texture and flavor.

Cassata

Ingredients:

For the Sponge Cake:

- 4 large eggs
- 3/4 cup granulated sugar
- 1 teaspoon vanilla extract
- 1 cup all-purpose flour
- 1 teaspoon baking powder
- Pinch of salt

For the Filling:

- 2 cups whole milk ricotta cheese, drained if necessary
- 1/2 cup powdered sugar, sifted
- 1 teaspoon vanilla extract
- 1/4 cup chopped candied fruit (such as orange peel, citron, or cherries)
- 1/4 cup chopped nuts (such as pistachios or almonds)
- 1/4 cup dark rum or orange liqueur (optional)

For Assembly and Decoration:

- Marzipan or almond paste
- Powdered sugar, for dusting
- Candied fruit and nuts for garnish

Instructions:

1. Make the Sponge Cake:
    - Preheat your oven to 350°F (175°C). Grease and flour a 9-inch round cake pan.
    - In a large mixing bowl, beat the eggs and granulated sugar together until pale and fluffy. Stir in the vanilla extract.
    - In a separate bowl, sift together the all-purpose flour, baking powder, and salt. Gradually fold the dry ingredients into the egg mixture until well combined.
    - Pour the batter into the prepared cake pan and smooth the top. Bake in the preheated oven for 25-30 minutes, or until a toothpick inserted into the center of the cake comes out clean.

- Remove the cake from the oven and let it cool completely in the pan before removing and slicing it horizontally into two layers.
2. Make the Filling:
   - In a mixing bowl, combine the ricotta cheese, powdered sugar, and vanilla extract. Mix until smooth and creamy.
   - Stir in the chopped candied fruit and nuts, and the rum or orange liqueur if using, until evenly distributed.
3. Assemble the Cassata:
   - Line the sides of a 9-inch springform pan with parchment paper. Place one layer of the sponge cake at the bottom of the pan.
   - Spread the ricotta filling evenly over the cake layer. Top with the second layer of sponge cake.
   - Press down gently to compact the layers. Cover the pan with plastic wrap and refrigerate for at least 4 hours, or preferably overnight, to allow the flavors to meld and the filling to set.
4. Decorate the Cassata:
   - Once chilled, remove the cassata from the springform pan and transfer it to a serving platter.
   - Roll out the marzipan or almond paste into a thin layer and carefully drape it over the top and sides of the cassata to cover completely.
   - Trim off any excess marzipan and smooth the surface with your hands or a cake smoother.
   - Decorate the cassata with powdered sugar, candied fruit, and nuts as desired.
5. Serve:
   - Slice the cassata into wedges and serve chilled. Enjoy this delicious and festive Sicilian dessert!

Tips:

- You can customize the filling by adding other ingredients such as chocolate chips, chopped dried fruit, or citrus zest.
- If you don't have marzipan or almond paste, you can use a simple icing made from powdered sugar and water to decorate the cassata.
- Cassata is best enjoyed chilled, so be sure to store any leftovers in the refrigerator. It will keep for up to 3 days.

Zeppole

Ingredients:

For the Dough:

- 1 cup water
- 1/2 cup unsalted butter
- 1 tablespoon granulated sugar
- 1/4 teaspoon salt
- 1 cup all-purpose flour
- 4 large eggs

For Frying and Serving:

- Vegetable oil, for frying
- Powdered sugar, for dusting

Instructions:

1. Prepare the Dough:
    - In a medium saucepan, combine water, butter, sugar, and salt. Bring to a boil over medium heat.
2. Add Flour:
    - Reduce the heat to low and add all-purpose flour to the saucepan. Stir vigorously with a wooden spoon until the mixture forms a ball and pulls away from the sides of the pan.
3. Cool the Dough:
    - Remove the saucepan from the heat and let it cool for a few minutes. Transfer the dough to a mixing bowl.
4. Add Eggs:
    - Add the eggs, one at a time, to the dough, beating well after each addition. The dough should be smooth and glossy.
5. Fry the Zeppole:
    - Heat vegetable oil in a deep pot or fryer to 375°F (190°C).
    - Using a spoon or a pastry bag fitted with a large star tip, drop spoonfuls of dough into the hot oil. Fry in batches, being careful not to overcrowd the pot.

- Fry the zeppole until they are golden brown and puffed up, about 3-4 minutes per batch. Use a slotted spoon to remove them from the oil and transfer them to a paper towel-lined plate to drain.
6. Serve:
    - Dust the warm zeppole with powdered sugar. Serve them immediately while they're still warm and crispy.

Variations:

- Filled Zeppole: After frying and cooling, you can fill the zeppole with your favorite filling, such as pastry cream, whipped cream, or Nutella. Use a piping bag fitted with a small tip to inject the filling into the center of each zeppola.
- Savory Zeppole: Instead of a sweet version, you can make savory zeppole by omitting the sugar in the dough and adding herbs, cheese, or garlic for flavor. Serve them as appetizers or alongside soups and salads.

Enjoy these delicious zeppole as a delightful treat for any occasion!

Amaretti

Ingredients:

- 2 cups almond flour (finely ground almonds)
- 1 cup granulated sugar
- 2 large egg whites
- 1 teaspoon almond extract
- Confectioners' sugar (powdered sugar), for dusting

Instructions:

1. Preheat the Oven:
    - Preheat your oven to 300°F (150°C). Line a baking sheet with parchment paper or a silicone baking mat.
2. Mix the Dough:
    - In a mixing bowl, combine the almond flour and granulated sugar. Stir until well mixed.
    - In a separate bowl, beat the egg whites until stiff peaks form.
    - Gently fold the beaten egg whites and almond extract into the almond flour mixture until a smooth, sticky dough forms.
3. Shape the Cookies:
    - Scoop out tablespoon-sized portions of dough and roll them into balls between your palms. Place the dough balls on the prepared baking sheet, spacing them a couple of inches apart.
4. Bake the Cookies:
    - Bake the amaretti cookies in the preheated oven for 15-18 minutes, or until they are lightly golden brown and firm to the touch.
    - Remove the baking sheet from the oven and let the cookies cool on the sheet for a few minutes before transferring them to a wire rack to cool completely.
5. Dust with Powdered Sugar:
    - Once the cookies are completely cool, dust them with confectioners' sugar (powdered sugar) using a fine-mesh sieve or sifter. This adds a decorative touch and enhances their sweetness.
6. Serve:
    - Serve the amaretti cookies as a delightful treat with coffee or tea, or enjoy them on their own as a sweet snack.

Tips:

- Make sure to use almond flour or finely ground almonds for the best texture in these cookies.
- If you prefer a smoother texture, you can use blanched almond flour instead of almond meal, which includes the almond skins.
- Store the amaretti cookies in an airtight container at room temperature for up to one week. They can also be frozen for longer storage.
- You can customize the flavor of these cookies by adding a pinch of ground cinnamon or lemon zest to the dough for extra depth of flavor.

Enjoy these homemade amaretti cookies, and savor their delicate almond flavor and delightful chewiness!

Semifreddo

Ingredients:

- 4 large eggs, separated
- 1/2 cup granulated sugar, divided
- 1 cup heavy cream
- 1 teaspoon vanilla extract
- Pinch of salt
- Optional flavorings: cocoa powder, espresso powder, fruit puree, chopped nuts, chocolate chips, etc.

Instructions:

1. Prepare the Pan:
    - Line a loaf pan with plastic wrap, leaving some overhang on the sides. This will make it easier to remove the semifreddo from the pan later.
2. Whip the Egg Whites:
    - In a clean, dry mixing bowl, beat the egg whites with an electric mixer until soft peaks form. Gradually add half of the granulated sugar and continue beating until stiff peaks form. Set aside.
3. Whip the Cream:
    - In another mixing bowl, whip the heavy cream with the remaining sugar and vanilla extract until soft peaks form.
4. Combine the Mixtures:
    - Gently fold the whipped cream into the beaten egg whites until well combined. Be careful not to deflate the mixture too much.
5. Add Flavorings (Optional):
    - If desired, fold in any flavorings or mix-ins at this point. For example, you could gently fold in cocoa powder for chocolate semifreddo or swirl in fruit puree for a fruity version.
6. Transfer to Pan:
    - Pour the semifreddo mixture into the prepared loaf pan and smooth the top with a spatula.
7. Freeze:
    - Cover the pan with plastic wrap and freeze the semifreddo for at least 4 hours, or preferably overnight, until firm.
8. Serve:

- When ready to serve, remove the semifreddo from the freezer and let it sit at room temperature for a few minutes to soften slightly. Use the plastic wrap overhang to lift the semifreddo out of the pan. Slice and serve.
9. Optional Garnish:
   - Garnish the slices of semifreddo with fresh fruit, chocolate sauce, caramel sauce, chopped nuts, or a dusting of cocoa powder, as desired.

Tips:

- Semifreddo is a versatile dessert, so feel free to get creative with flavorings and mix-ins. Just be sure not to add too much liquid, as it can affect the texture.
- For a fancier presentation, you can layer different flavors of semifreddo in the loaf pan before freezing.
- If you don't have a loaf pan, you can use individual ramekins or molds instead.

Enjoy this elegant and delicious Italian dessert that's perfect for any occasion!

Budino

Ingredients:

- 2 cups whole milk
- 1/2 cup granulated sugar
- 3 large egg yolks
- 1/4 cup cornstarch
- 1 teaspoon vanilla extract
- Pinch of salt
- Optional: 1/4 cup cocoa powder for chocolate budino

Instructions:

1. Prepare the Base:
    - In a saucepan, heat the milk over medium heat until it just begins to simmer. Remove from heat and set aside.
2. Whisk Egg Yolks:
    - In a mixing bowl, whisk together the granulated sugar and egg yolks until pale and creamy.
3. Add Cornstarch:
    - Gradually whisk in the cornstarch until smooth and well combined.
4. Temper the Eggs:
    - Gradually pour the hot milk into the egg yolk mixture, whisking constantly to temper the eggs and prevent them from curdling.
5. Cook the Mixture:
    - Return the mixture to the saucepan and place it over medium heat. Cook, stirring constantly with a wooden spoon or silicone spatula, until the mixture thickens and coats the back of the spoon. This will take about 5-7 minutes.
6. Flavor the Budino:
    - Remove the saucepan from the heat and stir in the vanilla extract and a pinch of salt. If making chocolate budino, whisk in the cocoa powder until well combined.
7. Strain (Optional):
    - For a smoother texture, you can strain the budino through a fine-mesh sieve into a clean bowl to remove any lumps or bits of cooked egg.
8. Chill:

- Transfer the budino to individual serving dishes or ramekins. Cover with plastic wrap, pressing it directly onto the surface of the budino to prevent a skin from forming. Chill in the refrigerator for at least 2 hours, or until set.

9. **Serve:**
    - Serve the budino chilled, either on its own or topped with caramel sauce, whipped cream, or fresh fruit.

Tips:

- To make caramel sauce for topping, simply heat equal parts sugar and water in a saucepan over medium heat until the sugar dissolves and turns amber in color. Remove from heat and whisk in heavy cream until smooth.
- For a richer flavor, you can use half-and-half or heavy cream instead of whole milk.
- Experiment with different flavorings such as almond extract, espresso powder, or citrus zest to customize your budino.

Enjoy this creamy and comforting Italian dessert that's sure to satisfy your sweet tooth!

Crostata

Ingredients:

For the Shortcrust Pastry:

- 2 cups all-purpose flour
- 1/2 cup granulated sugar
- 1/4 teaspoon salt
- 1/2 cup cold unsalted butter, cut into small cubes
- 1 large egg
- 1 teaspoon vanilla extract

For the Filling:

- 1 cup fruit preserves or jam (such as apricot, raspberry, or cherry)
- 2 cups fresh fruit (such as sliced peaches, berries, or plums)

Instructions:

1. Prepare the Shortcrust Pastry:
    - In a large mixing bowl, whisk together the all-purpose flour, granulated sugar, and salt.
    - Add the cold cubed butter to the flour mixture. Using your fingertips or a pastry cutter, work the butter into the flour until the mixture resembles coarse crumbs and the butter is evenly distributed.
    - In a small bowl, lightly beat the egg with the vanilla extract. Add the egg mixture to the flour mixture and gently knead until the dough comes together. Be careful not to overwork the dough.
    - Shape the dough into a disk, wrap it in plastic wrap, and refrigerate for at least 30 minutes to chill.
2. Preheat the Oven:
    - Preheat your oven to 375°F (190°C). Line a baking sheet with parchment paper or a silicone baking mat.
3. Roll Out the Dough:
    - On a lightly floured surface, roll out the chilled dough into a circle about 1/8 inch thick. Carefully transfer the rolled-out dough to the prepared baking sheet.
4. Fill the Crostata:

- Spread the fruit preserves or jam evenly over the center of the rolled-out dough, leaving a border of about 1 1/2 inches around the edges.
- Arrange the fresh fruit on top of the preserves or jam, overlapping slightly if necessary.

5. Fold the Edges:
   - Fold the edges of the dough up and over the filling, pleating as needed to create a rustic border.
6. Bake the Crostata:
   - Bake the crostata in the preheated oven for 30-35 minutes, or until the crust is golden brown and the fruit is bubbling.
7. Cool and Serve:
   - Remove the crostata from the oven and let it cool on the baking sheet for 10-15 minutes before transferring it to a wire rack to cool completely.
   - Serve the crostata warm or at room temperature, optionally dusted with powdered sugar.

Tips:

- You can customize the filling of the crostata based on your preference and seasonal fruit availability. Experiment with different fruit combinations and flavors of preserves or jam.
- For added flavor, you can sprinkle the edges of the crostata with turbinado sugar before baking.
- Serve the crostata with a dollop of whipped cream or a scoop of vanilla ice cream for an extra special treat.

Enjoy this delicious and versatile Italian dessert that's perfect for any occasion!

Ricotta Cheesecake

Ingredients:

For the Crust:

- 1 1/2 cups graham cracker crumbs (about 10-12 whole graham crackers)
- 1/4 cup granulated sugar
- 1/2 cup unsalted butter, melted

For the Filling:

- 2 lbs (about 4 cups) whole milk ricotta cheese, drained if necessary
- 1 cup granulated sugar
- 4 large eggs
- 1/4 cup all-purpose flour
- 1 teaspoon vanilla extract
- Zest of 1 lemon
- Pinch of salt

Instructions:

1. Preheat the Oven:
    - Preheat your oven to 325°F (160°C). Grease a 9-inch springform pan with butter or non-stick cooking spray.
2. Make the Crust:
    - In a mixing bowl, combine the graham cracker crumbs, granulated sugar, and melted butter. Mix until the crumbs are evenly coated with butter.
    - Press the mixture firmly into the bottom of the prepared springform pan, using the back of a spoon or a flat-bottomed glass to create an even layer. Bake the crust in the preheated oven for 10 minutes. Remove from the oven and let it cool while you prepare the filling.
3. Make the Filling:
    - In a large mixing bowl, beat the ricotta cheese and granulated sugar together until smooth and creamy.
    - Add the eggs one at a time, mixing well after each addition.
    - Stir in the all-purpose flour, vanilla extract, lemon zest, and a pinch of salt, mixing until the batter is smooth and well combined.
4. Assemble and Bake:

- Pour the filling over the cooled crust in the springform pan, smoothing the top with a spatula.
- Place the springform pan on a baking sheet to catch any drips, then transfer it to the preheated oven.
- Bake the cheesecake for 60-70 minutes, or until the edges are set and the center is slightly jiggly.
- Turn off the oven and leave the cheesecake inside with the oven door slightly ajar for about 1 hour to cool gradually. This helps prevent cracking.
- After cooling in the oven, transfer the cheesecake to a wire rack to cool completely. Once cooled, refrigerate the cheesecake for at least 4 hours, or overnight, to chill and set.

5. Serve:
    - Before serving, run a knife around the edges of the springform pan to loosen the cheesecake. Remove the outer ring of the pan.
    - Slice the cheesecake into wedges and serve chilled. Optionally, garnish with fresh berries, whipped cream, or a dusting of powdered sugar.

Tips:

- Make sure the ricotta cheese is well drained to avoid excess moisture in the cheesecake.
- For extra flavor, you can add a tablespoon of lemon juice or a splash of liqueur such as amaretto or rum to the filling.
- Ricotta cheesecake is delicious on its own, but you can also serve it with fruit compote, chocolate sauce, or caramel sauce for added sweetness.

Enjoy this creamy and indulgent ricotta cheesecake as a delightful dessert for any occasion!

Panettone

Ingredients:

For the Sponge:

- 1/2 cup (120ml) warm water
- 1 tablespoon (15g) active dry yeast
- 1/2 cup (65g) all-purpose flour

For the Dough:

- 4 large eggs, at room temperature
- 4 large egg yolks, at room temperature
- 1 cup (200g) granulated sugar
- 1 tablespoon vanilla extract
- Zest of 1 lemon
- Zest of 1 orange
- 1/2 cup (120ml) warm milk
- 1 cup (225g) unsalted butter, softened
- 4 cups (500g) all-purpose flour
- 1 teaspoon salt
- 1 cup mixed candied fruit, chopped
- 1/2 cup golden raisins
- Butter and flour, for greasing the panettone molds
- Pearl sugar or sliced almonds, for topping (optional)

Instructions:

1. Prepare the Sponge:
    - In a small bowl, combine the warm water and yeast. Let it sit for 5-10 minutes, or until frothy.
    - Stir in 1/2 cup of flour until well combined. Cover the bowl with plastic wrap and let it rest in a warm place for about 30 minutes, or until doubled in size.
2. Make the Dough:
    - In the bowl of a stand mixer fitted with the paddle attachment, beat the eggs, egg yolks, sugar, vanilla extract, lemon zest, and orange zest until pale and fluffy.

- Gradually add the warm milk and softened butter, mixing until well combined.
- Switch to the dough hook attachment. Gradually add the sponge mixture to the egg mixture, mixing until incorporated.
- In a separate bowl, whisk together the flour and salt. Gradually add the flour mixture to the dough, mixing on low speed until a soft, sticky dough forms.
- Stir in the candied fruit and golden raisins until evenly distributed.

3. First Rise:
   - Transfer the dough to a large greased bowl. Cover with plastic wrap and let it rise in a warm place for about 2 hours, or until doubled in size.
4. Prepare the Molds:
   - Grease the panettone molds with butter and dust them with flour to prevent sticking.
5. Shape the Dough:
   - Punch down the dough and transfer it to a lightly floured surface. Divide the dough into portions and shape each portion into a ball.
   - Place each dough ball into the prepared panettone molds. Cover with a clean kitchen towel and let them rise in a warm place for another 2 hours, or until doubled in size.
6. Second Rise and Preheat Oven:
   - Preheat your oven to 350°F (175°C) during the last 30 minutes of rising.
   - Optionally, brush the tops of the panettone with beaten egg and sprinkle with pearl sugar or sliced almonds.
7. Bake the Panettone:
   - Bake the panettone in the preheated oven for 30-40 minutes, or until golden brown and a toothpick inserted into the center comes out clean.
   - If the tops start to brown too quickly, cover them loosely with aluminum foil.
8. Cool and Serve:
   - Remove the panettone from the oven and let them cool in the molds for 10 minutes before transferring them to a wire rack to cool completely.
   - Serve the panettone sliced and enjoy!

Making panettone at home requires some planning and attention to detail, but the homemade version is sure to impress with its rich flavor and airy texture. Adjustments to the recipe can be made based on personal preference, such as using different types of candied fruit or adding nuts. Enjoy your homemade panettone as a festive treat during the holiday season or any time of the year!

Pandoro

Ingredients:

- 4 cups all-purpose flour
- ½ cup granulated sugar
- 1 teaspoon salt
- 1 package (2 ¼ teaspoons) active dry yeast
- ½ cup warm milk
- 4 large eggs, at room temperature
- ½ cup unsalted butter, softened
- 1 teaspoon vanilla extract
- Zest of 1 lemon
- Zest of 1 orange
- Powdered sugar, for dusting

Instructions:

1. Activate the yeast: In a small bowl, dissolve the yeast in warm milk and let it sit for about 5-10 minutes until it becomes frothy.
2. Prepare the dough: In a large mixing bowl, combine the flour, granulated sugar, and salt. Make a well in the center and add the activated yeast mixture, eggs, softened butter, vanilla extract, lemon zest, and orange zest. Mix until a dough forms.
3. Knead the dough: Turn the dough out onto a floured surface and knead it for about 10-15 minutes, or until it becomes smooth and elastic. You can also use a stand mixer with a dough hook attachment for this step.
4. First rise: Place the dough in a greased bowl, cover it with a clean kitchen towel or plastic wrap, and let it rise in a warm place for about 1-2 hours, or until it doubles in size.
5. Shape the Pandoro: After the dough has risen, punch it down to release the air bubbles. Divide the dough into two equal portions. Roll each portion into a ball and then flatten each ball into a disc. Stack the discs on top of each other, slightly off-center, to create a tree-like shape. Place the shaped dough into a Pandoro mold or a tall, narrow cake pan lined with parchment paper.
6. Second rise: Cover the shaped dough again and let it rise for another 2-3 hours, or until it doubles in size and fills the mold or pan.

7. Bake the Pandoro: Preheat your oven to 350°F (175°C). Bake the Pandoro for about 30-40 minutes, or until it is golden brown and a toothpick inserted into the center comes out clean.
8. Cool and dust: Allow the Pandoro to cool in the pan for about 10-15 minutes, then transfer it to a wire rack to cool completely. Once cooled, dust the Pandoro generously with powdered sugar before serving.

Enjoy your homemade Pandoro!

Struffoli

Ingredients:

- 3 cups all-purpose flour
- 4 large eggs
- 2 tablespoons granulated sugar
- 2 tablespoons unsalted butter, melted
- 1 teaspoon vanilla extract
- 1/4 teaspoon salt
- Vegetable oil, for frying
- 1 cup honey
- Candied fruits or colored sprinkles, for garnish

Instructions:

1. Prepare the dough: In a large mixing bowl, combine the flour, eggs, granulated sugar, melted butter, vanilla extract, and salt. Mix until a dough forms. If the dough is too dry, you can add a tablespoon of water at a time until it comes together.
2. Knead the dough: Turn the dough out onto a floured surface and knead it for about 5-10 minutes, or until it becomes smooth and elastic.
3. Shape the dough balls: Divide the dough into small pieces and roll each piece into thin ropes, about 1/4 inch in diameter. Cut the ropes into small pieces, about 1/2 inch long. Roll each piece into a small ball between your palms.
4. Fry the dough balls: In a large, deep skillet or pot, heat vegetable oil to 350°F (175°C). Fry the dough balls in batches until they are golden brown and puffed up, about 2-3 minutes per batch. Use a slotted spoon to transfer the fried dough balls to a paper towel-lined plate to drain excess oil.
5. Coat with honey: In a separate saucepan, heat the honey over low heat until it becomes thin and runny. Add the fried dough balls to the warm honey and stir until they are evenly coated.
6. Form the Struffoli: Transfer the honey-coated dough balls to a serving plate or platter. Using wet hands or a spoon, shape them into a mound or wreath-like shape.
7. Garnish: Decorate the Struffoli with candied fruits or colored sprinkles while the honey is still warm so they stick to the surface.
8. Serve: Allow the Struffoli to cool slightly before serving. They can be enjoyed warm or at room temperature.

Enjoy your delicious Struffoli! It's a festive treat that's perfect for sharing with family and friends.

Zuppa Inglese

Ingredients:

For the sponge cake:

- 6 large eggs, separated
- 1 cup granulated sugar
- 1 cup all-purpose flour
- 1 teaspoon vanilla extract

For the custard:

- 2 cups whole milk
- 4 large egg yolks
- 1/2 cup granulated sugar
- 1/4 cup cornstarch
- 1 teaspoon vanilla extract
- 1/4 cup rum or your preferred liqueur

For assembling:

- 1 cup heavy cream
- 2 tablespoons powdered sugar
- Cocoa powder, for dusting

Instructions:

1. Prepare the sponge cake: Preheat your oven to 350°F (175°C). Grease and flour a 9x13 inch baking dish.
2. In a large mixing bowl, beat the egg yolks with half of the sugar until pale and thick. Stir in the vanilla extract.
3. In another clean bowl, beat the egg whites until soft peaks form. Gradually add the remaining sugar and continue beating until stiff peaks form.
4. Gently fold the beaten egg whites into the egg yolk mixture. Sift the flour over the batter and fold it in gently until just combined.
5. Pour the batter into the prepared baking dish and spread it evenly. Bake for about 20-25 minutes, or until a toothpick inserted into the center comes out clean. Let the sponge cake cool completely.
6. Prepare the custard: In a saucepan, heat the milk over medium heat until steaming but not boiling.

7. In a separate bowl, whisk together the egg yolks, sugar, and cornstarch until smooth and pale.
8. Slowly pour the hot milk into the egg yolk mixture, whisking constantly to prevent curdling. Return the mixture to the saucepan and cook over medium heat, stirring constantly, until thickened.
9. Remove the custard from the heat and stir in the vanilla extract and rum. Let it cool completely.
10. Assemble the Zuppa Inglese: Cut the sponge cake into small squares or rectangles. Arrange a layer of sponge cake pieces in the bottom of a trifle dish or serving bowl.
11. Spoon a layer of custard over the sponge cake. Repeat the layers until all the cake and custard are used, ending with a layer of custard on top.
12. In a separate bowl, whip the heavy cream with powdered sugar until stiff peaks form. Spread the whipped cream over the top of the custard layer.
13. Cover the Zuppa Inglese with plastic wrap and refrigerate for at least 4 hours, or overnight, to allow the flavors to meld.
14. Before serving, dust the top of the Zuppa Inglese with cocoa powder for garnish. Enjoy this decadent Italian dessert!

Zuppa Inglese is a delightful dessert that's perfect for special occasions or any time you want to indulge in a rich and creamy treat. Buon appetito!

Bomboloni

Ingredients:

For the dough:

- 3 1/2 cups all-purpose flour
- 1/2 cup granulated sugar
- 1 teaspoon salt
- 1 packet (2 1/4 teaspoons) active dry yeast
- 1 cup warm milk
- 2 large eggs
- 4 tablespoons unsalted butter, softened
- 1 teaspoon vanilla extract
- Vegetable oil, for frying

For the filling (optional):

- Your choice of jam, custard, Nutella, or pastry cream

For coating:

- Granulated sugar or powdered sugar

Instructions:

1. Activate the yeast: In a small bowl, dissolve the yeast in warm milk and let it sit for about 5-10 minutes until it becomes frothy.
2. Prepare the dough: In a large mixing bowl, combine the flour, sugar, and salt. Make a well in the center and add the activated yeast mixture, eggs, softened butter, and vanilla extract. Mix until a dough forms.
3. Knead the dough: Turn the dough out onto a floured surface and knead it for about 5-10 minutes, or until it becomes smooth and elastic. You can also use a stand mixer with a dough hook attachment for this step.
4. First rise: Place the dough in a greased bowl, cover it with a clean kitchen towel or plastic wrap, and let it rise in a warm place for about 1-2 hours, or until it doubles in size.
5. Shape the bomboloni: After the dough has risen, punch it down to release the air bubbles. Roll the dough out on a floured surface to about 1/2 inch thickness. Use a round cookie cutter or glass to cut out circles of dough. Place a small spoonful

of your chosen filling in the center of half of the circles. Top each filled circle with another circle of dough and pinch the edges to seal.
6. Second rise: Place the filled bomboloni on a parchment-lined baking sheet, cover them with a clean kitchen towel, and let them rise for another 30-45 minutes, or until they puff up slightly.
7. Fry the bomboloni: In a large, deep skillet or pot, heat vegetable oil to 350°F (175°C). Fry the bomboloni in batches until they are golden brown on both sides, about 2-3 minutes per side. Use a slotted spoon to transfer them to a paper towel-lined plate to drain excess oil.
8. Coat with sugar: While the bomboloni are still warm, roll them in granulated sugar or dust them with powdered sugar until they are evenly coated.
9. Serve: Enjoy your homemade bomboloni warm or at room temperature. They're best eaten the day they're made, but you can store any leftovers in an airtight container for a day or two.

Enjoy these delicious Italian doughnuts as a special treat for breakfast, dessert, or any time you're craving something sweet!

Torta Caprese

Ingredients:

- 1 3/4 cups (200g) almond flour or finely ground almonds
- 1 1/4 cups (250g) granulated sugar
- 200g dark chocolate (at least 70% cocoa), chopped
- 1 cup (225g) unsalted butter, cubed
- 4 large eggs, separated
- 1 teaspoon vanilla extract
- Pinch of salt
- Powdered sugar, for dusting (optional)
- Sliced almonds, for garnish (optional)

Instructions:

1. Preheat oven and prepare pan: Preheat your oven to 325°F (160°C). Grease a 9-inch (23cm) springform pan and line the bottom with parchment paper.
2. Melt chocolate and butter: In a heatproof bowl set over a pot of simmering water (double boiler method), melt the chopped chocolate and cubed butter together, stirring occasionally until smooth. Alternatively, you can melt them in the microwave in short intervals, stirring in between, until smooth. Remove from heat and let cool slightly.
3. Mix almond flour and sugar: In a large mixing bowl, whisk together the almond flour and granulated sugar until well combined.
4. Add melted chocolate mixture: Gradually pour the melted chocolate and butter mixture into the almond flour mixture, stirring until smooth and well combined. Allow the mixture to cool slightly.
5. Add egg yolks and vanilla: Beat the egg yolks and vanilla extract into the chocolate mixture until fully incorporated.
6. Beat egg whites: In a separate clean mixing bowl, using an electric mixer, beat the egg whites with a pinch of salt until stiff peaks form.
7. Fold in egg whites: Gently fold the beaten egg whites into the chocolate mixture in two or three additions until no streaks of egg whites remain.
8. Transfer to pan and bake: Pour the batter into the prepared springform pan and spread it evenly. Bake in the preheated oven for about 40-45 minutes, or until the top is set and a toothpick inserted into the center comes out with a few moist crumbs attached.

9. Cool and serve: Allow the Torta Caprese to cool in the pan for about 10-15 minutes, then remove it from the pan and transfer it to a wire rack to cool completely. Dust with powdered sugar and garnish with sliced almonds, if desired, before serving.
10. Serve: Slice and serve the Torta Caprese at room temperature. It's delicious on its own or with a dollop of whipped cream or a scoop of vanilla ice cream.

Enjoy this decadent and gluten-free Italian chocolate cake as a delightful dessert for any occasion!

Pizzelle

Ingredients:

- 2 cups (250g) all-purpose flour
- 1 teaspoon baking powder
- 3/4 cup (150g) granulated sugar
- 1/2 cup (1 stick or 113g) unsalted butter, melted and cooled
- 3 large eggs
- 1 tablespoon vanilla extract
- Optional: Anise extract or other flavorings such as almond or lemon zest
- Optional: Powdered sugar, for dusting

Instructions:

1. Preheat Pizzelle maker: Preheat your Pizzelle maker according to the manufacturer's instructions.
2. Prepare batter: In a medium mixing bowl, whisk together the flour and baking powder.
3. In a separate large mixing bowl, beat the eggs and granulated sugar together until pale and fluffy.
4. Gradually add the melted butter and vanilla extract (and any optional flavorings) to the egg mixture, beating until well combined.
5. Gradually add the dry ingredients to the wet ingredients, mixing until a smooth batter forms. The batter should have a thick consistency similar to cake batter.
6. Cook Pizzelle: Lightly grease the Pizzelle maker with cooking spray or brush it with melted butter. Drop a tablespoon of batter onto the center of each pattern on the Pizzelle maker. Close the lid and cook according to the manufacturer's instructions, usually for about 45-60 seconds, or until the Pizzelle are golden brown and crispy.
7. Use a fork or a spatula to carefully remove the Pizzelle from the Pizzelle maker and transfer them to a wire rack to cool completely. They will crisp up as they cool.
8. Repeat: Continue cooking the remaining batter in batches, greasing the Pizzelle maker as needed.
9. Optional: Once cooled, dust the Pizzelle with powdered sugar for an extra touch of sweetness.

10. Serve and store: Serve the Pizzelle as they are or pair them with coffee, tea, or ice cream. Store any leftovers in an airtight container at room temperature for up to a week.

Enjoy these delicious and beautifully patterned Italian cookies as a festive treat or anytime you crave a sweet snack!

Torta della Nonna

Ingredients:

For the pastry:

- 2 cups (250g) all-purpose flour
- 1/2 cup (100g) granulated sugar
- 1/2 cup (1 stick or 113g) unsalted butter, cold and cubed
- 1 large egg
- 1 large egg yolk
- Zest of 1 lemon
- 1 teaspoon baking powder
- Pinch of salt

For the pastry cream:

- 2 cups (480ml) whole milk
- 4 large egg yolks
- 1/2 cup (100g) granulated sugar
- 1/4 cup (30g) all-purpose flour
- 1 teaspoon vanilla extract
- Zest of 1 lemon

For assembling and topping:

- 1/4 cup (30g) pine nuts
- Powdered sugar, for dusting

Instructions:

1. Prepare the pastry: In a large mixing bowl, combine the flour, granulated sugar, lemon zest, baking powder, and salt. Add the cold, cubed butter and use your fingers or a pastry cutter to cut it into the dry ingredients until the mixture resembles coarse crumbs.
2. Add the egg and egg yolk to the mixture and gently knead until the dough comes together. Shape the dough into a ball, wrap it in plastic wrap, and refrigerate it for at least 30 minutes.
3. Preheat the oven: Preheat your oven to 350°F (175°C). Grease a 9-inch (23cm) tart pan with a removable bottom.

4. Prepare the pastry cream: In a saucepan, heat the milk over medium heat until steaming but not boiling.
5. In a separate bowl, whisk together the egg yolks, granulated sugar, and flour until smooth and pale. Gradually pour the hot milk into the egg yolk mixture, whisking constantly to prevent curdling.
6. Return the mixture to the saucepan and cook over medium heat, stirring constantly, until thickened. Remove from heat and stir in the vanilla extract and lemon zest. Let the pastry cream cool completely.
7. Assemble the Torta della Nonna: Roll out two-thirds of the pastry dough on a lightly floured surface to fit the bottom and sides of the prepared tart pan. Press the dough into the pan and trim any excess.
8. Pour the cooled pastry cream into the tart shell and spread it out evenly.
9. Roll out the remaining pastry dough and place it over the top of the tart. Trim any excess dough and press the edges to seal.
10. Add pine nuts and bake: Sprinkle the pine nuts over the top of the tart. Bake in the preheated oven for about 30-35 minutes, or until the pastry is golden brown and the filling is set.
11. Cool and serve: Allow the Torta della Nonna to cool in the pan for about 10-15 minutes, then remove it from the pan and transfer it to a wire rack to cool completely. Dust with powdered sugar before serving.
12. Serve: Slice and serve the Torta della Nonna at room temperature. Enjoy this classic Italian dessert with a cup of coffee or tea!

This Torta della Nonna recipe is sure to impress with its creamy filling and delicate pastry crust. Buon appetito!

Maritozzi

Ingredients:

For the buns:

- 4 cups (500g) all-purpose flour
- 1/2 cup (100g) granulated sugar
- 1/2 teaspoon salt
- 2 1/4 teaspoons (1 packet) active dry yeast
- 1/2 cup (120ml) warm milk
- 1/2 cup (120ml) warm water
- 1/2 cup (1 stick or 113g) unsalted butter, softened
- 2 large eggs
- Zest of 1 lemon or orange
- 1 teaspoon vanilla extract

For the filling (optional):

- Whipped cream

For brushing:

- 1 egg, beaten

For garnish:

- Powdered sugar, for dusting

Instructions:

1. Activate the yeast: In a small bowl, dissolve the yeast in warm milk and let it sit for about 5-10 minutes until it becomes frothy.
2. Prepare the dough: In a large mixing bowl, combine the flour, sugar, and salt. Make a well in the center and add the activated yeast mixture, warm water, softened butter, eggs, lemon or orange zest, and vanilla extract. Mix until a dough forms.
3. Knead the dough: Turn the dough out onto a floured surface and knead it for about 10-15 minutes, or until it becomes smooth and elastic.
4. First rise: Place the dough in a greased bowl, cover it with a clean kitchen towel or plastic wrap, and let it rise in a warm place for about 1-2 hours, or until it doubles in size.

5. Shape the buns: After the dough has risen, punch it down to release the air bubbles. Divide the dough into equal portions and shape each portion into a ball. Place the balls on a parchment-lined baking sheet, leaving some space between them.
6. Second rise: Cover the shaped buns with a clean kitchen towel and let them rise for another 30-45 minutes, or until they double in size.
7. Preheat the oven: Preheat your oven to 350°F (175°C).
8. Brush with egg wash: Brush the risen buns with beaten egg to give them a shiny appearance when baked.
9. Bake the buns: Bake the buns in the preheated oven for about 15-20 minutes, or until they are golden brown and sound hollow when tapped on the bottom.
10. Cool and fill (if desired): Allow the buns to cool completely on a wire rack. Once cooled, you can slice them horizontally and fill them with whipped cream if desired.
11. Garnish and serve: Dust the filled buns with powdered sugar before serving. Enjoy your homemade Maritozzi with a cup of coffee or tea!

Maritozzi are a delightful treat with their soft texture and hint of sweetness. They're perfect for indulging in a taste of Italy at breakfast or as a snack any time of day. Buon appetito!

Torrone

Ingredients:

- 1 cup (240ml) honey
- 1 cup (200g) granulated sugar
- 2 large egg whites
- 2 1/2 cups (300g) whole almonds or hazelnuts, toasted and coarsely chopped
- 1 teaspoon vanilla extract
- Zest of 1 lemon or orange (optional)
- Edible rice paper sheets (optional, for wrapping)

Instructions:

1. Prepare the pan: Line a 9x9 inch (23x23cm) baking dish with parchment paper, leaving some overhang on the sides for easy removal later. If using edible rice paper, place a sheet on the bottom of the dish.
2. Toast the nuts: Spread the almonds or hazelnuts evenly on a baking sheet and toast them in a preheated oven at 350°F (175°C) for about 8-10 minutes, or until lightly golden and fragrant. Let them cool slightly, then coarsely chop them.
3. Prepare the syrup: In a medium saucepan, combine the honey and granulated sugar. Heat the mixture over medium heat, stirring constantly, until the sugar is dissolved and the mixture reaches 300°F (150°C) on a candy thermometer (hard crack stage).
4. Beat egg whites: While the syrup is heating, in a separate bowl, beat the egg whites until stiff peaks form.
5. Combine ingredients: Once the syrup reaches the desired temperature, remove it from the heat and gradually pour it into the beaten egg whites while continuing to beat at medium speed.
6. Add nuts and flavorings: Stir in the chopped nuts, vanilla extract, and citrus zest (if using), mixing until well combined and the mixture starts to thicken slightly.
7. Pour into prepared dish: Immediately pour the torrone mixture into the prepared baking dish, spreading it out evenly with a spatula.
8. Let cool and set: Allow the torrone to cool and set at room temperature for several hours or overnight. Once completely cooled and firm, lift the torrone out of the dish using the parchment paper overhang and transfer it to a cutting board.
9. Cut into pieces: Use a sharp knife to cut the torrone into small rectangles or squares, depending on your preference.

10. Wrap (optional): If desired, wrap the individual pieces of torrone in edible rice paper to help prevent sticking and for a traditional presentation.
11. Serve or store: Serve the torrone immediately, or store it in an airtight container at room temperature for up to several weeks.

Enjoy your homemade torrone as a sweet treat or gift it to friends and family during the holiday season!

Granita

Ingredients:

- 4 cups (960ml) water
- 1 cup (200g) granulated sugar
- Flavoring of your choice (e.g., fruit juice, coffee, tea, wine)
- Optional: Fresh fruit or mint leaves for garnish

Instructions:

1. Make simple syrup: In a saucepan, combine the water and granulated sugar. Heat the mixture over medium heat, stirring occasionally, until the sugar is completely dissolved. Remove the saucepan from heat and let the simple syrup cool to room temperature.
2. Choose your flavor: Decide on the flavor for your granita. You can use fruit juice (such as lemon, orange, or berry), brewed coffee or tea (such as espresso, green tea, or chamomile), wine (such as rosé or prosecco), or any other liquid you prefer.
3. Mix flavoring with syrup: Once the simple syrup has cooled, stir in your chosen flavoring until well combined. You can adjust the flavoring to taste, depending on how strong you want the flavor to be.
4. Pour into a shallow dish: Pour the flavored syrup into a shallow dish or baking pan. The shallower the dish, the faster the granita will freeze.
5. Freeze and scrape: Place the dish in the freezer and let the mixture freeze for about 1-2 hours, or until it starts to set around the edges. Use a fork to scrape and stir the mixture, breaking up any ice crystals that have formed. Continue to freeze and scrape every 30 minutes to 1 hour, until the entire mixture is frozen and flaky.
6. Serve: Once the granita is completely frozen and has a fluffy texture, it's ready to serve. Spoon the granita into serving dishes and garnish with fresh fruit or mint leaves if desired.
7. Enjoy: Serve the granita immediately as a refreshing dessert or snack. It's perfect for hot summer days or as a light and cooling treat after a meal.

Experiment with different flavor combinations and have fun creating your own unique granita recipes!

Frittelle di Carnevale

Ingredients:

- 1 cup (125g) all-purpose flour
- 2 tablespoons granulated sugar
- 1 teaspoon baking powder
- Pinch of salt
- 2 large eggs
- 1/2 cup (120ml) milk
- 1 tablespoon melted butter or vegetable oil
- Zest of 1 lemon or orange (optional)
- 1/4 cup (40g) raisins or chopped dried fruit (optional)
- Vegetable oil, for frying
- Powdered sugar, for dusting

Instructions:

1. Prepare the batter: In a large mixing bowl, whisk together the flour, granulated sugar, baking powder, and salt.
2. In a separate bowl, beat the eggs with the milk, melted butter or oil, and citrus zest (if using) until well combined.
3. Gradually add the wet ingredients to the dry ingredients, stirring until a smooth batter forms. If using, fold in the raisins or chopped dried fruit.
4. Fry the frittelle: In a deep skillet or pot, heat vegetable oil to 350°F (175°C) over medium heat. Use a thermometer to ensure the oil reaches the correct temperature.
5. Drop spoonfuls of batter into the hot oil, being careful not to overcrowd the pan. Fry the frittelle in batches for about 2-3 minutes per side, or until golden brown and cooked through.
6. Use a slotted spoon to transfer the fried frittelle to a paper towel-lined plate to drain excess oil.
7. Dust with powdered sugar: Once the frittelle are slightly cooled but still warm, dust them generously with powdered sugar.
8. Serve: Serve the Frittelle di Carnevale warm as a delicious treat for Carnival celebrations or anytime you crave a sweet snack.

Enjoy these delightful Carnival fritters with a cup of coffee or tea, and indulge in the festive spirit of Italian Carnival traditions!

Biscotti Regina

Ingredients:

- 2 cups (250g) all-purpose flour
- 1/2 cup (100g) granulated sugar
- 1/2 cup (1 stick or 113g) unsalted butter, softened
- 1 large egg
- 1 teaspoon baking powder
- 1/4 teaspoon salt
- 1 teaspoon vanilla extract
- 1/2 cup (75g) sesame seeds, toasted

Instructions:

1. Preheat oven: Preheat your oven to 350°F (175°C). Line a baking sheet with parchment paper or silicone baking mat.
2. Toast sesame seeds: Spread the sesame seeds in a single layer on a baking sheet and toast them in the preheated oven for about 5-7 minutes, or until lightly golden and fragrant. Keep an eye on them as they can burn quickly. Once toasted, remove them from the oven and let them cool.
3. Cream butter and sugar: In a large mixing bowl, cream together the softened butter and granulated sugar until light and fluffy.
4. Add egg and vanilla: Beat in the egg and vanilla extract until well combined.
5. Mix dry ingredients: In a separate bowl, whisk together the flour, baking powder, and salt.
6. Combine wet and dry ingredients: Gradually add the dry ingredients to the wet ingredients, mixing until a dough forms. Fold in the toasted sesame seeds until evenly distributed throughout the dough.
7. Shape dough: Divide the dough into small portions and roll each portion into a ball, about 1 inch (2.5cm) in diameter. Roll each ball in additional sesame seeds to coat them generously.
8. Bake: Place the coated dough balls on the prepared baking sheet, spacing them about 2 inches (5cm) apart. Gently flatten each ball with the palm of your hand.
9. Bake in the preheated oven for about 12-15 minutes, or until the cookies are lightly golden brown around the edges.
10. Cool and serve: Allow the Biscotti Regina to cool on the baking sheet for a few minutes, then transfer them to a wire rack to cool completely. Once cooled, store them in an airtight container at room temperature.

Enjoy these delicious Biscotti Regina as a delightful snack or treat alongside your favorite hot beverage!

Torta Mimosa

Ingredients:

For the sponge cake:

- 6 large eggs, separated
- 1 cup (200g) granulated sugar
- 1 cup (120g) all-purpose flour
- 1 teaspoon baking powder
- Zest of 1 lemon or orange
- Pinch of salt

For the filling:

- 2 cups (480ml) heavy cream
- 1/2 cup (100g) granulated sugar
- Zest of 1 lemon or orange
- 1 teaspoon vanilla extract
- 1/4 cup (60ml) limoncello or orange liqueur (optional)

For garnish:

- Powdered sugar
- Candied flowers or fresh flowers (optional)

Instructions:

1. Preheat oven and prepare pans: Preheat your oven to 350°F (175°C). Grease and flour two 9-inch (23cm) round cake pans or line them with parchment paper.
2. Prepare the sponge cake: In a large mixing bowl, beat the egg yolks with half of the sugar until pale and thick. Stir in the lemon or orange zest.
3. In a separate bowl, sift together the flour and baking powder.
4. In another clean bowl, beat the egg whites with a pinch of salt until soft peaks form. Gradually add the remaining sugar and continue beating until stiff peaks form.
5. Gently fold the beaten egg whites into the egg yolk mixture until just combined. Gradually fold in the sifted flour mixture until no streaks remain.
6. Divide the batter evenly between the prepared cake pans and smooth the tops with a spatula. Bake in the preheated oven for about 20-25 minutes, or until the cakes are lightly golden brown and spring back when lightly touched.

7. Cool the cakes: Allow the cakes to cool in the pans for a few minutes, then transfer them to a wire rack to cool completely.
8. Prepare the filling: In a large mixing bowl, beat the heavy cream with the sugar, lemon or orange zest, and vanilla extract until stiff peaks form. If using, fold in the limoncello or orange liqueur.
9. Assemble the Torta Mimosa: Once the cakes are completely cooled, use a serrated knife to slice each cake horizontally into two layers, creating a total of four layers.
10. Place one cake layer on a serving plate or cake stand. Spread a layer of the whipped cream filling over the cake layer. Repeat with the remaining cake layers and filling, ending with a layer of whipped cream on top.
11. Garnish: Dust the top of the Torta Mimosa with powdered sugar. Decorate with candied flowers or fresh flowers if desired.
12. Chill and serve: Refrigerate the Torta Mimosa for at least 1-2 hours before serving to allow the flavors to meld and the filling to set. Slice and serve chilled.

Enjoy this delightful Torta Mimosa as a festive and elegant dessert to celebrate International Women's Day or any special occasion!

Croccante

Ingredients:

- 1 cup (200g) granulated sugar
- 1 cup (200g) mixed nuts (such as almonds, hazelnuts, or peanuts), roughly chopped
- 2 tablespoons water
- 1 tablespoon unsalted butter
- Optional: 1 teaspoon vanilla extract or a pinch of salt

Instructions:

1. Prepare a baking sheet: Line a baking sheet with parchment paper or a silicone baking mat. Set it aside.
2. Toast the nuts (optional): If using raw nuts, spread them evenly on a baking sheet and toast them in a preheated oven at 350°F (175°C) for about 8-10 minutes, or until lightly golden and fragrant. Keep an eye on them as they can burn quickly. Once toasted, remove them from the oven and let them cool.
3. Cook the sugar: In a heavy-bottomed saucepan, combine the granulated sugar and water over medium heat. Stir until the sugar is completely dissolved.
4. Caramelize the sugar: Once the sugar has dissolved, stop stirring and let the mixture come to a boil. Allow it to boil without stirring until it reaches a golden caramel color. This process may take about 5-7 minutes.
5. Add nuts and butter: Once the caramel reaches the desired color, quickly stir in the chopped nuts and unsalted butter. Stir until the butter is melted and the nuts are evenly coated with the caramel.
6. Flavoring (optional): If desired, stir in vanilla extract or a pinch of salt to enhance the flavor of the croccante.
7. Transfer to baking sheet: Immediately pour the hot caramel-nut mixture onto the prepared baking sheet. Use a spatula or spoon to spread it out into an even layer.
8. Cool and set: Let the croccante cool completely at room temperature until it hardens and sets, usually about 30 minutes to 1 hour.
9. Break into pieces: Once the croccante is completely cooled and set, break it into pieces using your hands or a knife.
10. Serve: Serve the croccante as a sweet and crunchy snack or dessert. It's perfect for enjoying on its own or as a topping for ice cream or other desserts.

Store any leftover croccante in an airtight container at room temperature for up to several days.

Enjoy the delightful combination of sweet caramelized sugar and crunchy nuts in this classic Italian treat!

Mostaccioli

Ingredients:

For the cookies:

- 3 cups (360g) all-purpose flour
- 1 cup (200g) granulated sugar
- 1/2 cup (50g) unsweetened cocoa powder
- 1 teaspoon baking powder
- 1/2 teaspoon baking soda
- 1/2 teaspoon ground cinnamon
- 1/4 teaspoon ground cloves
- 1/4 teaspoon ground nutmeg
- Pinch of salt
- 1/2 cup (120ml) vegetable oil
- 1/2 cup (120ml) milk
- 1/4 cup (60ml) honey
- 1 teaspoon vanilla extract
- 1/2 cup (75g) chopped nuts (such as almonds or walnuts), optional

For the glaze (optional):

- 1 cup (120g) powdered sugar
- 2-3 tablespoons milk or water
- 1/2 teaspoon vanilla extract

Instructions:

1. Preheat oven and prepare baking sheets: Preheat your oven to 350°F (175°C). Line baking sheets with parchment paper or silicone baking mats.
2. Mix dry ingredients: In a large mixing bowl, whisk together the flour, sugar, cocoa powder, baking powder, baking soda, spices, and salt until well combined.
3. Add wet ingredients: In a separate bowl, whisk together the vegetable oil, milk, honey, and vanilla extract until smooth.
4. Combine wet and dry ingredients: Gradually add the wet ingredients to the dry ingredients, mixing until a dough forms. If using, fold in the chopped nuts until evenly distributed.

5. Shape the cookies: Divide the dough into small portions and roll each portion into a log about 1/2 inch (1.5cm) in diameter. Cut the logs into diamond shapes or elongated ovals.
6. Bake: Place the shaped cookies on the prepared baking sheets, spacing them about 1 inch (2.5cm) apart. Bake in the preheated oven for about 10-12 minutes, or until the cookies are set and slightly firm to the touch.
7. Cool: Allow the cookies to cool on the baking sheets for a few minutes, then transfer them to a wire rack to cool completely.
8. Prepare the glaze (optional): In a small bowl, whisk together the powdered sugar, milk or water, and vanilla extract until smooth. Drizzle the glaze over the cooled cookies or dip the tops of the cookies into the glaze.
9. Let the glaze set: Allow the glaze to set before serving or storing the cookies.
10. Serve or store: Enjoy the Mostaccioli cookies as a sweet treat for festive occasions or as a delightful snack. Store any leftover cookies in an airtight container at room temperature for up to several days.

These Mostaccioli cookies are sure to delight with their rich cocoa flavor and aromatic spices. Buon appetito!

Fiadone

Ingredients:

- 1 pound (450g) fresh ricotta cheese
- 3 large eggs
- 3/4 cup (150g) granulated sugar
- Zest of 1 lemon
- 1 tablespoon orange blossom water (optional)
- Confectioners' sugar, for dusting (optional)

Instructions:

1. Preheat the oven: Preheat your oven to 350°F (175°C). Grease a 9-inch (23cm) round cake pan with butter or non-stick cooking spray.
2. Prepare the ricotta: Place the ricotta cheese in a fine-mesh strainer or cheesecloth-lined colander set over a bowl. Let it drain for about 30 minutes to remove excess moisture.
3. Prepare the batter: In a large mixing bowl, beat the eggs and granulated sugar together until well combined and slightly frothy. Stir in the lemon zest and orange blossom water, if using.
4. Add the ricotta: Gently fold the drained ricotta cheese into the egg mixture until smooth and well incorporated.
5. Bake the Fiadone: Pour the batter into the prepared cake pan and spread it out evenly with a spatula. Bake in the preheated oven for about 40-45 minutes, or until the Fiadone is set and lightly golden brown on top.
6. Cool and serve: Allow the Fiadone to cool in the pan for about 10-15 minutes, then remove it from the pan and transfer it to a wire rack to cool completely. Once cooled, dust the top with confectioners' sugar if desired.
7. Slice and serve: Slice the Fiadone into wedges and serve at room temperature. Enjoy this creamy and slightly sweet Italian dessert as a delightful treat!

Fiadone is often enjoyed on its own or with a drizzle of honey or a dollop of fruit preserves. It's a versatile dessert that can be served for various occasions or enjoyed as a simple indulgence. Buon appetito!

Pinolata

Ingredients:

- 2 cups (250g) all-purpose flour
- 1 cup (200g) granulated sugar
- 1 cup (200g) unsalted butter, softened
- 4 large eggs
- 1/2 cup (60g) pine nuts
- 1 teaspoon vanilla extract
- Zest of 1 lemon
- 1/4 cup (60ml) milk
- 1 teaspoon baking powder
- Pinch of salt

Instructions:

1. Preheat oven and prepare pan: Preheat your oven to 350°F (175°C). Grease and flour a 9-inch (23cm) round cake pan or line it with parchment paper.
2. Toast pine nuts: In a dry skillet over medium heat, toast the pine nuts until lightly golden and fragrant, stirring frequently to prevent burning. Remove from heat and let them cool.
3. Prepare batter: In a large mixing bowl, cream together the softened butter and granulated sugar until light and fluffy. Add the eggs, one at a time, beating well after each addition. Stir in the vanilla extract and lemon zest.
4. Combine dry ingredients: In a separate bowl, sift together the flour, baking powder, and salt.
5. Add dry ingredients to wet: Gradually add the dry ingredients to the wet ingredients, alternating with the milk, and mix until just combined. Be careful not to overmix.
6. Fold in pine nuts: Gently fold the toasted pine nuts into the batter until evenly distributed.
7. Bake: Pour the batter into the prepared cake pan and spread it out evenly with a spatula. Bake in the preheated oven for about 30-35 minutes, or until a toothpick inserted into the center comes out clean.
8. Cool: Allow the Pinolata to cool in the pan for about 10 minutes, then transfer it to a wire rack to cool completely.
9. Serve: Once cooled, slice the Pinolata into wedges and serve. Enjoy this delightful Tuscan dessert with a cup of coffee or tea!

Pinolata is a wonderful treat that showcases the rich flavor of pine nuts and is perfect for serving at any gathering or as a special dessert for your family and friends. Buon appetito!

Panforte

Ingredients:

- 1 cup (140g) whole almonds
- 1 cup (140g) whole hazelnuts
- 1/2 cup (100g) candied orange peel, chopped
- 1/2 cup (100g) candied lemon peel, chopped
- 1/2 cup (80g) dried figs, chopped
- 1/2 cup (80g) dried apricots, chopped
- 1/2 cup (80g) dried cherries or cranberries
- 1 cup (140g) all-purpose flour
- 1 teaspoon ground cinnamon
- 1/2 teaspoon ground nutmeg
- 1/4 teaspoon ground cloves
- 1/4 teaspoon ground black pepper
- Pinch of salt
- 1 cup (240ml) honey
- 3/4 cup (150g) granulated sugar
- Powdered sugar, for dusting

Instructions:

1. Preheat oven and prepare pan: Preheat your oven to 325°F (160°C). Line the bottom of a 9-inch (23cm) round cake pan with parchment paper and lightly grease the sides.
2. Toast nuts: Spread the almonds and hazelnuts on a baking sheet and toast them in the preheated oven for about 10-12 minutes, or until lightly golden and fragrant. Let them cool, then roughly chop them.
3. Mix fruits and nuts: In a large mixing bowl, combine the toasted nuts, candied orange peel, candied lemon peel, dried figs, dried apricots, and dried cherries or cranberries. Toss to combine.
4. Prepare flour and spices: In a separate bowl, whisk together the all-purpose flour, ground cinnamon, ground nutmeg, ground cloves, ground black pepper, and pinch of salt.
5. Combine flour mixture with fruits and nuts: Add the flour mixture to the bowl of fruits and nuts, and toss until the fruits and nuts are evenly coated.

6. Heat honey and sugar: In a saucepan, heat the honey and granulated sugar over medium heat, stirring occasionally, until the sugar is completely dissolved and the mixture is smooth.
7. Combine ingredients: Pour the hot honey-sugar mixture over the fruits and nuts, stirring until everything is evenly coated and combined.
8. Bake: Transfer the mixture to the prepared cake pan, pressing it down firmly with the back of a spoon or spatula to compact it.
9. Bake in the oven: Bake in the preheated oven for about 30-35 minutes, or until the top is lightly golden brown and set.
10. Cool and dust with powdered sugar: Remove the panforte from the oven and let it cool completely in the pan. Once cooled, remove it from the pan and dust the top with powdered sugar.
11. Slice and serve: Slice the panforte into thin wedges and serve. Enjoy this delicious and festive Italian dessert with a cup of coffee or tea!

Panforte is a delightful treat with its rich flavors and chewy texture, and it's perfect for sharing with friends and family during the holiday season or any time of year. Buon appetito!

Tartufo

Ingredients:

For the gelato filling:

- 2 cups (480ml) heavy cream
- 1 cup (240ml) whole milk
- 3/4 cup (150g) granulated sugar
- 4 large egg yolks
- 1 teaspoon vanilla extract
- 1/2 cup (120ml) chocolate liqueur (such as Kahlua or Frangelico)
- 1/2 cup (75g) chopped nuts (such as hazelnuts or almonds), optional

For the chocolate shell:

- 8 ounces (225g) dark chocolate, chopped
- 2 tablespoons vegetable oil or coconut oil
- Cocoa powder, for dusting

For garnish (optional):

- Whipped cream
- Chocolate shavings
- Chopped nuts
- Maraschino cherries

Instructions:

1. Prepare the gelato filling: In a saucepan, combine the heavy cream, whole milk, and granulated sugar. Heat the mixture over medium heat, stirring occasionally, until it begins to simmer. Remove from heat.
2. In a separate bowl, whisk the egg yolks until smooth. Gradually pour the hot cream mixture into the egg yolks, whisking constantly to temper the eggs.
3. Return the mixture to the saucepan and cook over low heat, stirring constantly, until it thickens slightly and coats the back of a spoon, about 5-7 minutes. Do not let it boil.
4. Remove the saucepan from heat and stir in the vanilla extract and chocolate liqueur. If using, fold in the chopped nuts. Let the mixture cool completely.

5. Form the gelato balls: Once the gelato mixture is cooled, use a small ice cream scoop or spoon to form balls of gelato. Place the balls on a parchment-lined baking sheet and freeze until firm, about 1-2 hours.
6. Make the chocolate shell: In a microwave-safe bowl, melt the chopped dark chocolate and vegetable oil in 30-second intervals, stirring between each interval, until smooth and fully melted.
7. Assemble the Tartufo: Remove the gelato balls from the freezer. Working quickly, dip each ball into the melted chocolate, coating it completely. Use a fork or spoon to lift the coated ball out of the chocolate and place it back on the parchment-lined baking sheet.
8. Freeze: Once all the gelato balls are coated in chocolate, return the baking sheet to the freezer and freeze the Tartufi until the chocolate shell is firm, about 1-2 hours.
9. Serve: Before serving, dust the Tartufi with cocoa powder. If desired, garnish with whipped cream, chocolate shavings, chopped nuts, or maraschino cherries.
10. Enjoy: Serve the Tartufi immediately as a decadent dessert. Buon appetito!

Tartufo is a delightful treat with its creamy gelato center and rich chocolate shell, making it the perfect indulgence for any occasion.

Sbrisolona

Ingredients:

- 2 cups (250g) all-purpose flour
- 1 cup (200g) granulated sugar
- 1 cup (100g) almond flour or finely ground almonds
- 1 cup (225g) cold unsalted butter, cut into small cubes
- 1/2 cup (50g) sliced almonds
- Zest of 1 lemon
- 1 teaspoon vanilla extract
- 1/2 teaspoon salt
- 1 large egg
- 1 tablespoon cold water

Instructions:

1. Preheat oven: Preheat your oven to 350°F (175°C). Line a baking sheet with parchment paper or a silicone baking mat.
2. Prepare the dough: In a large mixing bowl, combine the all-purpose flour, granulated sugar, almond flour (or finely ground almonds), sliced almonds, lemon zest, vanilla extract, and salt. Mix until well combined.
3. Add butter: Add the cold cubed butter to the dry ingredients. Using your fingertips or a pastry cutter, rub the butter into the flour mixture until it resembles coarse crumbs and the butter is evenly distributed.
4. Add egg and water: In a small bowl, whisk together the egg and cold water. Pour the egg mixture into the flour mixture and gently mix until the dough comes together. Be careful not to overmix.
5. Shape the dough: Transfer the dough to the prepared baking sheet. Use your hands to press the dough into a round, flat disc, about 1 inch (2.5cm) thick. It's okay if the edges are a bit uneven.
6. Bake: Bake the Sbrisolona in the preheated oven for 30-35 minutes, or until it is golden brown and firm to the touch.
7. Cool and serve: Remove the Sbrisolona from the oven and let it cool on the baking sheet for about 10 minutes. Transfer it to a wire rack to cool completely before slicing.
8. Slice and enjoy: Once cooled, slice the Sbrisolona into wedges or irregular pieces. Serve and enjoy with a cup of coffee or dessert wine.

Sbrisolona is known for its crumbly texture, so don't worry if it breaks apart a bit when slicing. That's part of its charm! This rustic Italian dessert is perfect for sharing with friends and family, especially during special occasions or as an afternoon treat. Buon appetito!

Castagnaccio

Ingredients:

- 2 cups (250g) chestnut flour
- 2 cups (480ml) water
- 1/4 cup (60ml) extra virgin olive oil, plus extra for greasing
- 1/2 cup (100g) granulated sugar
- 1/2 cup (75g) pine nuts
- 1/4 cup (40g) raisins (optional)
- 1 tablespoon fresh rosemary leaves
- Pinch of salt

Instructions:

1. Preheat oven: Preheat your oven to 375°F (190°C). Grease a 9-inch (23cm) round cake pan with olive oil.
2. Prepare the batter: In a mixing bowl, whisk together the chestnut flour and water until smooth and well combined. Add the olive oil, granulated sugar, and a pinch of salt, and mix until the batter is smooth.
3. Add pine nuts and raisins: Stir in the pine nuts and raisins (if using) until evenly distributed throughout the batter.
4. Transfer to pan: Pour the batter into the prepared cake pan and spread it out evenly with a spatula.
5. Sprinkle with rosemary: Scatter the fresh rosemary leaves over the top of the batter.
6. Bake: Bake the Castagnaccio in the preheated oven for 30-35 minutes, or until the top is firm and lightly golden brown.
7. Cool and serve: Remove the Castagnaccio from the oven and let it cool in the pan for a few minutes. Transfer it to a wire rack to cool completely before slicing.
8. Slice and enjoy: Once cooled, slice the Castagnaccio into wedges or squares. Serve and enjoy at room temperature.

Castagnaccio is best enjoyed within a day or two of baking. It pairs well with a glass of Vin Santo, a sweet dessert wine from Tuscany, or a cup of espresso. Its unique flavor and texture make it a delightful treat for autumn and winter gatherings or any time you're craving a taste of traditional Italian cuisine. Buon appetito!

Baci di Dama

Ingredients:

For the cookies:

- 1 cup (120g) hazelnuts, toasted and finely ground
- 1 cup (120g) all-purpose flour
- 1/2 cup (100g) granulated sugar
- 1/2 cup (115g) unsalted butter, softened
- Pinch of salt
- 1/2 teaspoon vanilla extract

For the filling:

- 3/4 cup (130g) semisweet chocolate chips or chopped chocolate
- 1/4 cup (60ml) heavy cream

Instructions:

1. Prepare hazelnuts: Preheat your oven to 350°F (175°C). Spread the hazelnuts in a single layer on a baking sheet and toast them in the preheated oven for about 10-12 minutes, or until fragrant and lightly golden brown. Remove from the oven and let them cool slightly. Once cooled, place the hazelnuts in a food processor and pulse until finely ground.
2. Make cookie dough: In a mixing bowl, cream together the softened butter and granulated sugar until light and fluffy. Add the vanilla extract and a pinch of salt, and mix until combined. Gradually add the ground hazelnuts and all-purpose flour, mixing until a smooth dough forms.
3. Form cookies: Shape the dough into small balls, about 1 teaspoon of dough for each cookie. Place the balls on a parchment-lined baking sheet, leaving some space between them.
4. Bake: Bake the cookies in the preheated oven for about 10-12 minutes, or until they are lightly golden brown around the edges. Remove from the oven and let them cool completely on the baking sheet.
5. Make chocolate filling: In a heatproof bowl, combine the semisweet chocolate chips or chopped chocolate with the heavy cream. Heat the mixture in the microwave or over a double boiler, stirring occasionally, until the chocolate is melted and the mixture is smooth.

6. Assemble Baci di Dama: Once the cookies are cooled, pair them up based on size. Spread a small amount of the chocolate filling on the flat side of one cookie, then gently press the flat side of another cookie on top to create a sandwich. Repeat with the remaining cookies.
7. Let the cookies set: Place the assembled cookies on a wire rack or baking sheet and let them sit at room temperature for about 30 minutes to allow the chocolate filling to set.
8. Serve and enjoy: Once the chocolate filling is set, serve the Baci di Dama cookies and enjoy their delicious hazelnut and chocolate flavor!

Baci di Dama are perfect for serving as a sweet treat with coffee or tea, or for gifting to friends and family on special occasions. Buon appetito!

Brutti ma Buoni

Ingredients:

- 3 large egg whites, at room temperature
- 1 cup (200g) granulated sugar
- 1 cup (120g) finely chopped hazelnuts or almonds
- 1 teaspoon vanilla extract
- Pinch of salt

Instructions:

1. Preheat oven: Preheat your oven to 300°F (150°C). Line a baking sheet with parchment paper or a silicone baking mat.
2. Prepare meringue: In a clean, dry mixing bowl, beat the egg whites with a pinch of salt using an electric mixer on medium speed until soft peaks form.
3. Add sugar: Gradually add the granulated sugar to the egg whites, a spoonful at a time, while continuing to beat on medium-high speed. Beat until the meringue is thick, glossy, and holds stiff peaks.
4. Fold in nuts and vanilla: Gently fold in the finely chopped hazelnuts or almonds and vanilla extract until evenly distributed throughout the meringue.
5. Shape cookies: Drop spoonfuls of the meringue mixture onto the prepared baking sheet, leaving some space between each cookie. The cookies will spread slightly as they bake, so keep that in mind when spacing them.
6. Bake: Bake the cookies in the preheated oven for about 20-25 minutes, or until they are firm to the touch and lightly golden brown.
7. Cool: Remove the cookies from the oven and let them cool on the baking sheet for a few minutes. Then, transfer them to a wire rack to cool completely.
8. Serve and enjoy: Once cooled, serve the Brutti ma Buoni cookies and enjoy their crispy exterior and chewy interior!

Brutti ma Buoni cookies are perfect for enjoying as a sweet treat with a cup of coffee or tea. They also make lovely homemade gifts for friends and family. Buon appetito!

Ciambellone

Ingredients:

- 3 cups (375g) all-purpose flour
- 1 1/2 cups (300g) granulated sugar
- 4 large eggs
- 1 cup (240ml) whole milk
- 1/2 cup (120ml) vegetable oil or melted butter
- Zest of 1 lemon or orange
- 2 teaspoons baking powder
- 1 teaspoon vanilla extract
- Pinch of salt
- Powdered sugar, for dusting (optional)

Instructions:

1. Preheat oven: Preheat your oven to 350°F (175°C). Grease and flour a 10-inch (25cm) bundt cake pan or a ring-shaped cake pan.
2. Mix dry ingredients: In a large mixing bowl, whisk together the all-purpose flour, granulated sugar, baking powder, and a pinch of salt until well combined.
3. Add wet ingredients: In another bowl, beat the eggs with the whole milk, vegetable oil (or melted butter), lemon or orange zest, and vanilla extract until smooth.
4. Combine wet and dry ingredients: Gradually add the wet ingredients to the dry ingredients, stirring until just combined. Be careful not to overmix.
5. Pour batter into pan: Pour the batter into the prepared bundt cake pan, spreading it out evenly with a spatula.
6. Bake: Bake in the preheated oven for about 45-50 minutes, or until a toothpick inserted into the center comes out clean and the top is golden brown.
7. Cool: Remove the ciambellone from the oven and let it cool in the pan for about 10 minutes. Then, carefully remove it from the pan and transfer it to a wire rack to cool completely.
8. Dust with powdered sugar: Once cooled, dust the ciambellone with powdered sugar, if desired, before serving.
9. Slice and enjoy: Slice the ciambellone into wedges and serve. Enjoy this simple and delicious Italian cake with a cup of coffee or tea!

Ciambellone is a versatile dessert that can be customized with different flavorings such as citrus zest, vanilla, or even chocolate chips. It's perfect for any occasion and is sure to be a hit with family and friends. Buon appetito!

Cantucci

Ingredients:

- 2 cups (250g) all-purpose flour
- 1 cup (200g) granulated sugar
- 1 teaspoon baking powder
- 1/4 teaspoon salt
- 3 large eggs
- 1 teaspoon vanilla extract
- Zest of 1 lemon
- 1 cup (150g) whole almonds, toasted

Instructions:

1. Preheat oven: Preheat your oven to 350°F (175°C). Line a baking sheet with parchment paper or a silicone baking mat.
2. Toast almonds: Spread the whole almonds in a single layer on a baking sheet and toast them in the preheated oven for about 8-10 minutes, or until lightly golden and fragrant. Let them cool, then roughly chop them.
3. Mix dry ingredients: In a large mixing bowl, whisk together the all-purpose flour, granulated sugar, baking powder, and salt until well combined.
4. Add wet ingredients: In a separate bowl, beat the eggs with the vanilla extract and lemon zest until well combined.
5. Combine ingredients: Gradually add the wet ingredients to the dry ingredients, stirring until a dough forms. Fold in the toasted almonds until evenly distributed throughout the dough.
6. Shape dough: Divide the dough in half. On a lightly floured surface, shape each half into a log about 12 inches (30cm) long and 2 inches (5cm) wide. Place the logs on the prepared baking sheet, spacing them apart.
7. Bake: Bake the logs in the preheated oven for about 25-30 minutes, or until they are firm to the touch and lightly golden brown.
8. Cool: Remove the baking sheet from the oven and let the logs cool on the baking sheet for about 10 minutes.
9. Slice: Using a sharp knife, slice the logs diagonally into 1/2-inch (1.5cm) thick slices.
10. Bake again: Place the slices cut side down on the baking sheet and return them to the oven. Bake for an additional 10-15 minutes, or until the cookies are crisp and golden brown.

11. Cool and serve: Remove the Cantucci from the oven and let them cool completely on a wire rack before serving. Enjoy these classic Italian cookies with a glass of Vin Santo or your favorite hot beverage!

Cantucci can be stored in an airtight container at room temperature for up to two weeks, making them a perfect homemade treat or gift for friends and family. Buon appetito!

Torta di Mele

Ingredients:

- 3 large apples (such as Granny Smith or Golden Delicious)
- 1 1/2 cups (190g) all-purpose flour
- 1/2 cup (100g) granulated sugar
- 1/2 cup (120ml) milk
- 1/3 cup (80ml) vegetable oil or melted butter
- 2 large eggs
- 2 teaspoons baking powder
- 1 teaspoon vanilla extract
- Zest of 1 lemon (optional)
- Pinch of salt
- Powdered sugar, for dusting (optional)
- Cinnamon, for dusting (optional)

Instructions:

1. Preheat oven: Preheat your oven to 350°F (175°C). Grease and flour a 9-inch (23cm) round cake pan or springform pan.
2. Prepare apples: Peel, core, and thinly slice the apples. You can sprinkle the slices with a little lemon juice to prevent browning if desired.
3. Mix dry ingredients: In a large mixing bowl, whisk together the all-purpose flour, granulated sugar, baking powder, and a pinch of salt until well combined.
4. Add wet ingredients: In another bowl, whisk together the milk, vegetable oil (or melted butter), eggs, and vanilla extract until smooth. Stir in the lemon zest if using.
5. Combine wet and dry ingredients: Gradually add the wet ingredients to the dry ingredients, mixing until just combined. Be careful not to overmix.
6. Assemble cake: Pour the batter into the prepared cake pan, spreading it out evenly with a spatula. Arrange the apple slices on top of the batter in a circular pattern, pressing them gently into the batter.
7. Bake: Bake in the preheated oven for about 35-40 minutes, or until the cake is golden brown and a toothpick inserted into the center comes out clean.
8. Cool and serve: Remove the cake from the oven and let it cool in the pan for about 10 minutes. Then, transfer it to a wire rack to cool completely. Dust the top with powdered sugar and/or cinnamon before serving if desired.

9. Slice and enjoy: Once cooled, slice the Torta di Mele into wedges and serve. Enjoy this classic Italian apple cake with a cup of coffee or tea!

Torta di Mele is a wonderful way to showcase the natural sweetness of apples in a delightful cake. It's perfect for serving as a dessert or as a sweet treat for any occasion. Buon appetito!

Torta Paradiso

Ingredients:

- 1 cup (225g) unsalted butter, softened, plus extra for greasing
- 1 1/2 cups (300g) granulated sugar
- 6 large eggs, separated
- 1 teaspoon vanilla extract
- Zest of 1 lemon
- Zest of 1 orange
- 2 cups (250g) cake flour
- 1 teaspoon baking powder
- Pinch of salt
- Powdered sugar, for dusting (optional)

Instructions:

1. Preheat oven: Preheat your oven to 350°F (175°C). Grease and flour a 9-inch (23cm) round cake pan or springform pan.
2. Cream butter and sugar: In a large mixing bowl, cream together the softened butter and granulated sugar until light and fluffy.
3. Add egg yolks and flavorings: Add the egg yolks one at a time, mixing well after each addition. Stir in the vanilla extract, lemon zest, and orange zest until combined.
4. Sift dry ingredients: In a separate bowl, sift together the cake flour, baking powder, and a pinch of salt.
5. Combine wet and dry ingredients: Gradually add the sifted dry ingredients to the wet ingredients, mixing until just combined.
6. Whip egg whites: In another clean mixing bowl, beat the egg whites until stiff peaks form.
7. Fold in egg whites: Gently fold the whipped egg whites into the cake batter until evenly incorporated. Be careful not to deflate the egg whites.
8. Bake: Pour the batter into the prepared cake pan and smooth the top with a spatula. Bake in the preheated oven for about 35-40 minutes, or until the cake is golden brown and a toothpick inserted into the center comes out clean.
9. Cool and serve: Remove the cake from the oven and let it cool in the pan for about 10 minutes. Then, transfer it to a wire rack to cool completely. Dust the top with powdered sugar before serving if desired.

10. Slice and enjoy: Once cooled, slice the Torta Paradiso into wedges and serve. Enjoy this delightful Italian cake with a cup of coffee or tea!

Torta Paradiso is a heavenly treat with its light and airy texture and subtle citrus flavor. It's perfect for any celebration or as a sweet indulgence for dessert. Buon appetito!

Baba al Limoncello

Ingredients:

For the baba:

- 2 1/4 teaspoons (1 packet) active dry yeast
- 1/4 cup (60ml) warm water (about 110°F/45°C)
- 2 cups (250g) all-purpose flour
- 3 large eggs, at room temperature
- 1/4 cup (50g) granulated sugar
- 1/4 cup (60ml) milk, at room temperature
- 1/4 cup (60g) unsalted butter, melted and cooled
- Zest of 1 lemon
- Pinch of salt

For the syrup:

- 1/2 cup (120ml) water
- 1/2 cup (100g) granulated sugar
- 1/2 cup (120ml) Limoncello liqueur
- Zest of 1 lemon (optional)

For serving (optional):

- Whipped cream
- Fresh berries

Instructions:

1. Activate yeast: In a small bowl, dissolve the active dry yeast in warm water. Let it sit for about 5-10 minutes, or until frothy.
2. Prepare dough: In a large mixing bowl, combine the all-purpose flour, granulated sugar, lemon zest, and a pinch of salt. Make a well in the center and add the activated yeast mixture, eggs, milk, and melted butter. Mix until a smooth dough forms. The dough will be soft and sticky.
3. First rise: Cover the bowl with plastic wrap or a clean kitchen towel and let the dough rise in a warm, draft-free place for about 1-2 hours, or until doubled in size.
4. Shape baba: Punch down the risen dough and divide it into equal portions. Shape each portion into small round balls and place them on a baking sheet lined with

parchment paper, leaving some space between each one. Cover loosely with plastic wrap and let them rise for another 30-45 minutes.
5. Bake: Preheat your oven to 350°F (175°C). Bake the baba in the preheated oven for about 15-20 minutes, or until they are golden brown and cooked through. Remove them from the oven and let them cool slightly.
6. Prepare syrup: While the baba are baking, make the syrup. In a saucepan, combine the water and granulated sugar over medium heat, stirring until the sugar is dissolved. Remove from heat and stir in the Limoncello liqueur and lemon zest, if using.
7. Soak baba: While the baba are still warm, place them in a shallow dish and pour the Limoncello syrup over them, allowing them to soak for at least 30 minutes to 1 hour, or until they have absorbed the syrup.
8. Serve: Serve the Baba al Limoncello with a dollop of whipped cream and fresh berries if desired. Enjoy this delightful Italian dessert with its lemony flavor and moist texture!

Baba al Limoncello is best served fresh but can be stored in an airtight container in the refrigerator for a day or two. Bring them to room temperature before serving for the best flavor and texture. Buon appetito!

Ricciarelli

Ingredients:

- 2 cups (200g) almond flour
- 1 cup (200g) granulated sugar
- 2 large egg whites
- Zest of 1 orange
- Zest of 1 lemon
- 1 teaspoon almond extract
- 1/2 cup (60g) powdered sugar, for dusting
- Additional powdered sugar, for rolling

Instructions:

1. Preheat oven: Preheat your oven to 325°F (160°C). Line a baking sheet with parchment paper.
2. Mix ingredients: In a large mixing bowl, combine the almond flour, granulated sugar, orange zest, lemon zest, and almond extract. Mix until well combined.
3. Whip egg whites: In a separate clean mixing bowl, beat the egg whites with an electric mixer until stiff peaks form.
4. Combine mixtures: Gently fold the whipped egg whites into the almond flour mixture until a soft dough forms. Be careful not to deflate the egg whites.
5. Shape cookies: Place some powdered sugar on a plate or shallow dish. Take small portions of the dough and roll them into balls between your hands. Roll each ball in powdered sugar to coat them completely.
6. Flatten cookies: Place the coated dough balls on the prepared baking sheet and gently flatten them slightly with your fingers to form oval-shaped cookies.
7. Bake: Bake the Ricciarelli in the preheated oven for about 15-18 minutes, or until they are lightly golden brown around the edges and set. The cookies will still be soft when you touch them.
8. Cool: Remove the cookies from the oven and let them cool on the baking sheet for a few minutes before transferring them to a wire rack to cool completely.
9. Dust with powdered sugar: Once cooled, dust the Ricciarelli with powdered sugar for an extra sweet touch.
10. Serve and enjoy: Serve the Ricciarelli cookies as a delightful treat with a cup of coffee or tea. Enjoy their soft and chewy texture and citrusy almond flavor!

Ricciarelli are best enjoyed within a few days of baking and can be stored in an airtight container at room temperature. They also make lovely homemade gifts for friends and family. Buon appetito!

Biancomangiare

Ingredients:

- 4 cups (960ml) whole milk
- 1/2 cup (100g) granulated sugar
- 1/2 cup (60g) cornstarch or rice flour
- 1 teaspoon almond extract (or vanilla extract)
- Sliced almonds, toasted (for garnish)
- Ground cinnamon or nutmeg (for garnish)
- Fresh berries or fruit compote (optional, for serving)

Instructions:

1. Prepare milk mixture: In a saucepan, combine the whole milk and granulated sugar. Heat the mixture over medium heat, stirring constantly, until the sugar is dissolved and the milk is hot but not boiling.
2. Thicken mixture: In a small bowl, whisk together the cornstarch or rice flour with a little bit of cold milk to create a slurry. Gradually whisk the slurry into the hot milk mixture, stirring constantly to prevent lumps from forming.
3. Cook mixture: Continue to cook the mixture over medium heat, stirring constantly, until it thickens and coats the back of a spoon, similar to the consistency of pudding. This usually takes about 5-7 minutes.
4. Flavor: Remove the saucepan from the heat and stir in the almond extract or vanilla extract. Taste and adjust the flavoring if necessary.
5. Chill: Pour the Biancomangiare mixture into individual serving dishes or a large serving bowl. Cover with plastic wrap, pressing the wrap directly onto the surface of the dessert to prevent a skin from forming. Chill in the refrigerator for at least 2-3 hours, or until set.
6. Serve: Once chilled and set, garnish the Biancomangiare with toasted sliced almonds and a sprinkle of ground cinnamon or nutmeg. Serve with fresh berries or fruit compote if desired.

Biancomangiare is a versatile dessert that can be enjoyed on its own or paired with a variety of toppings. It's a light and refreshing treat that's perfect for any occasion. Buon appetito!

Gubana

Ingredients:

For the dough:

- 4 cups (500g) all-purpose flour
- 1/2 cup (100g) granulated sugar
- 1/2 cup (120ml) warm milk
- 2 large eggs, beaten
- 1/2 cup (115g) unsalted butter, melted and cooled
- Zest of 1 lemon
- Pinch of salt

For the filling:

- 1 cup (150g) mixed nuts (such as walnuts, almonds, and hazelnuts), chopped
- 1/2 cup (75g) raisins or other dried fruits, chopped
- 1/2 cup (100g) granulated sugar
- 1/4 cup (60ml) rum or brandy
- 1/2 cup (120ml) warm milk
- 2 tablespoons unsweetened cocoa powder
- 1 teaspoon ground cinnamon
- 1/2 teaspoon vanilla extract
- Zest of 1 orange

For brushing:

- 2 tablespoons melted unsalted butter
- 2 tablespoons granulated sugar

Instructions:

1. Prepare the dough: In a large mixing bowl, combine the warm milk and sugar. Sprinkle the yeast over the mixture and let it sit for about 5-10 minutes, or until foamy. Add the beaten eggs, melted butter, lemon zest, and a pinch of salt. Gradually add the flour, mixing until a soft dough forms. Knead the dough on a floured surface for about 5-7 minutes, or until smooth and elastic. Place the dough in a greased bowl, cover with a clean kitchen towel, and let it rise in a warm, draft-free place for about 1-2 hours, or until doubled in size.

2. Prepare the filling: In a medium mixing bowl, combine the chopped nuts, raisins, sugar, rum or brandy, warm milk, cocoa powder, cinnamon, vanilla extract, and orange zest. Mix until well combined and set aside.
3. Assemble the Gubana: Punch down the risen dough and roll it out on a lightly floured surface into a large rectangle, about 1/4 inch (0.6 cm) thick. Spread the filling evenly over the dough, leaving a small border around the edges. Starting from one long side, roll up the dough tightly into a log. Place the log seam side down and shape it into a spiral. Transfer the Gubana to a parchment-lined baking sheet.
4. Final rise: Cover the Gubana with a clean kitchen towel and let it rise in a warm, draft-free place for about 30-45 minutes, or until slightly puffed.
5. Bake: Preheat your oven to 350°F (175°C). Brush the top of the Gubana with melted butter and sprinkle with granulated sugar. Bake in the preheated oven for about 35-45 minutes, or until golden brown and cooked through. If the top begins to brown too quickly, cover loosely with aluminum foil.
6. Cool and serve: Remove the Gubana from the oven and let it cool on the baking sheet for about 10-15 minutes before transferring it to a wire rack to cool completely. Once cooled, slice and serve the Gubana. Enjoy this delightful and aromatic pastry with a cup of coffee or tea!

Gubana is a special treat that requires some effort to make, but the result is truly worth it. Its rich and flavorful filling encased in soft, sweet bread makes it a wonderful dessert to enjoy during festive occasions or as a special indulgence any time of the year. Buon appetito!

Bustrengo

Ingredients:

- 1 cup (200g) cornmeal
- 1 cup (125g) all-purpose flour
- 1 cup (200g) granulated sugar
- 1/2 cup (100g) unsalted butter, melted
- 1 cup (240ml) milk
- 1/2 cup (75g) raisins or other dried fruits
- 1/2 cup (60g) chopped nuts (such as walnuts or almonds)
- Zest of 1 lemon
- Zest of 1 orange
- 1 teaspoon ground cinnamon
- 1/2 teaspoon ground nutmeg
- Pinch of salt

Instructions:

1. Preheat oven: Preheat your oven to 350°F (175°C). Grease a 9-inch (23cm) square baking dish or cake pan.
2. Mix dry ingredients: In a large mixing bowl, combine the cornmeal, all-purpose flour, granulated sugar, ground cinnamon, ground nutmeg, and a pinch of salt.
3. Add wet ingredients: Gradually add the melted butter and milk to the dry ingredients, stirring until well combined and smooth.
4. Fold in fruits and nuts: Stir in the raisins or other dried fruits, chopped nuts, lemon zest, and orange zest until evenly distributed throughout the batter.
5. Pour into pan: Pour the batter into the prepared baking dish, spreading it out evenly with a spatula.
6. Bake: Bake in the preheated oven for about 30-35 minutes, or until the Bustrengo is golden brown on top and cooked through. A toothpick inserted into the center should come out clean.
7. Cool and serve: Remove the Bustrengo from the oven and let it cool in the pan for about 10-15 minutes before slicing and serving. Enjoy this rustic Italian dessert warm or at room temperature with a dusting of powdered sugar, if desired.

Bustrengo is a simple and comforting dessert that's perfect for serving to family and friends on chilly days. Its hearty texture and warming spices make it a delightful treat to enjoy during the fall and winter seasons. Buon appetito!

Migliaccio

Ingredients:

- 1 cup (200g) fine semolina flour
- 2 cups (480ml) whole milk
- 1 cup (200g) granulated sugar
- 1 cup (250g) ricotta cheese
- 4 large eggs
- Zest of 1 lemon (or 1 teaspoon vanilla extract)
- 1/4 cup (60ml) limoncello liqueur (optional)
- Butter or cooking spray, for greasing

Instructions:

1. Preheat oven: Preheat your oven to 350°F (175°C). Grease a 9-inch (23cm) round cake pan or baking dish with butter or cooking spray.
2. Cook semolina: In a saucepan, bring the whole milk to a gentle simmer over medium heat. Gradually whisk in the semolina flour, stirring constantly to prevent lumps from forming. Cook the mixture, stirring continuously, for about 5-7 minutes, or until thickened and smooth. Remove from heat and let it cool slightly.
3. Prepare batter: In a large mixing bowl, whisk together the granulated sugar, ricotta cheese, eggs, and lemon zest (or vanilla extract) until well combined. Gradually whisk in the cooked semolina mixture until smooth. If using, stir in the limoncello liqueur.
4. Bake: Pour the batter into the prepared cake pan or baking dish, spreading it out evenly with a spatula. Tap the pan gently on the counter to remove any air bubbles. Bake in the preheated oven for about 40-45 minutes, or until the Migliaccio is set and lightly golden brown on top.
5. Cool and serve: Remove the Migliaccio from the oven and let it cool in the pan for about 10-15 minutes before slicing and serving. Serve warm or at room temperature, dusted with powdered sugar if desired.

Migliaccio can be served as a dessert or a sweet snack, and it pairs well with a cup of coffee or tea. Its creamy texture and delicate flavor make it a delightful treat for any occasion. Buon appetito!

Pignolata

Ingredients:

For the dough:

- 3 cups (375g) all-purpose flour
- 3 large eggs
- 1/4 cup (50g) granulated sugar
- 1/4 cup (60ml) dry white wine or Marsala wine
- 1/4 cup (60ml) vegetable oil
- Zest of 1 lemon
- Pinch of salt
- Vegetable oil, for frying

For the honey glaze:

- 1 cup (240ml) honey
- Zest of 1 lemon or orange (optional)
- Candied citrus peel or sprinkles (for decoration, optional)

Instructions:

1. Prepare dough: In a large mixing bowl, combine the all-purpose flour, granulated sugar, lemon zest, and a pinch of salt. Make a well in the center and add the eggs, dry white wine, and vegetable oil. Mix until a smooth dough forms. If the dough is too dry, you can add a little more wine or water as needed.
2. Knead dough: Turn the dough out onto a lightly floured surface and knead it for about 5-7 minutes, or until smooth and elastic. Shape the dough into a ball and let it rest for about 30 minutes, covered with a clean kitchen towel or plastic wrap.
3. Shape dough balls: After the dough has rested, pinch off small pieces of dough and roll them into small balls, about the size of a marble.
4. Fry dough balls: In a large, deep skillet or pot, heat vegetable oil over medium heat until it reaches about 350°F (175°C). Carefully add the dough balls in batches, making sure not to overcrowd the pan. Fry them for about 2-3 minutes, or until golden brown and cooked through. Use a slotted spoon to transfer the fried dough balls to a paper towel-lined plate to drain excess oil. Repeat until all dough balls are fried.

5. Prepare honey glaze: In a separate saucepan, heat the honey over low heat until it becomes thin and runny. Stir in the lemon or orange zest, if using.
6. Assemble Pignolata: Once all the dough balls are fried and drained, transfer them to a large mixing bowl. Pour the warm honey glaze over the dough balls and toss gently to coat them evenly.
7. Shape and decorate: Arrange the glazed dough balls into a mound or ring shape on a serving platter. You can also sprinkle them with candied citrus peel or colored sprinkles for decoration, if desired.
8. Serve: Let the Pignolata cool and set for a few hours before serving. Once set, it's ready to be enjoyed as a delicious and festive sweet treat!

Pignolata is a delightful dessert that's perfect for sharing with family and friends during special occasions. Its crispy, fried dough balls coated in sweet honey glaze are sure to be a hit with everyone. Buon appetito!

Sanguinaccio Dolce

Ingredients:

- 2 cups (480ml) whole milk
- 1/2 cup (100g) granulated sugar
- 1/3 cup (40g) unsweetened cocoa powder
- 1/4 cup (30g) cornstarch or potato starch
- 1 teaspoon ground cinnamon (optional)
- 1/2 teaspoon vanilla extract
- Pinch of salt
- Grated zest of 1 orange or lemon (optional)
- Chopped nuts or candied orange peel, for garnish (optional)

Instructions:

1. Mix dry ingredients: In a mixing bowl, whisk together the granulated sugar, unsweetened cocoa powder, cornstarch (or potato starch), ground cinnamon (if using), and a pinch of salt until well combined.
2. Heat milk: In a saucepan, heat the whole milk over medium heat until it begins to steam. Do not let it boil.
3. Combine ingredients: Gradually whisk the dry ingredient mixture into the hot milk, stirring constantly to prevent lumps from forming.
4. Cook pudding: Continue to cook the mixture over medium heat, stirring constantly, until it thickens and coats the back of a spoon, similar to the consistency of pudding. This usually takes about 5-7 minutes.
5. Flavor: Remove the saucepan from the heat and stir in the vanilla extract and grated orange or lemon zest (if using). Taste and adjust the flavoring if necessary.
6. Cool and serve: Transfer the Sanguinaccio Dolce to serving bowls or ramekins. Let it cool slightly before serving. You can serve it warm or chilled, garnished with chopped nuts or candied orange peel if desired.

Sanguinaccio Dolce is a rich and comforting dessert that's perfect for indulging in during the colder months. Its creamy texture and chocolatey flavor make it a favorite treat for many Italians, especially during Carnival season. Buon appetito!